MW01196850

Santa Fe Hispanic Culture: Preserving Identity in a Tourist Town
University of New Mexico Press, 2004

With its use of academic research, interviews and Lovato's own analysis of the situation, *Santa Fe Hispanic Culture* offers a good introduction to the subject and will be especially valuable to newcomers who want some insight into what makes Santa Fe tick.

—*Albuquerque Journal*

A book all Westerners should read and consider, since the cultural identity of Santa Fe is a part of Western history that we cannot afford to lose.

—*Roundup* Magazine

A thought-provoking and sobering counterpoint to the city's tourist mystique.

—*Revista,* journal of the Southwest Mission Research Center

Santa Fe Hispanic Culture should easily win the City Different's chamber of commerce endorsement.

—La Herencia del Norte

Elvis Romero and Fiesta de Santa Fe, Featuring Zozobra's Great Escape
Museum of New Mexico Press, 2011

2012 New Mexico-Arizona Book Award Finalist
2012 Pubwest Book Design Award

Lovato captures many of the historical and ritual goings-on of the Fiesta de Santa Fe with text and photographs from the Palace of the Governors Photo Archives. He also includes a thrilling fictional tale as the centerpiece of the book, about a boy named Elvis Romero and his cousin and best friend, a girl named Pepa. In the story, Elvis and Pepa decide to liberate Zozobra from his appointed fate, and hatch a plan to hide him. The author zeroes in on his own childhood fears and worries about Zozobra's safety through his central characters, who are amalgams of the kids he grew up with in Santa Fe. Lovato examines, in a playful and sentimental way, the feelings of empathy he and other children had and still have for Zozobra.

—Pasatiempo (magazine of the *Santa Fe New Mexican*)

More than a colorful retelling of a young boy's realization, the book is also a narrative of the past. Black and white photographs of the fiesta's past complete the story [and] also complement the last part of the book, a Fiesta de Santa Fe timeline which chronicles the start of the Santa Fe Fiesta from 1625 to present day.

—*New Mexico Daily Lobo*

A lovingly crafted tome featuring stories about Fiesta de Santa Fe and idyllic black-and-white photography.

—*Santa Fe Reporter*

The Big Book of Blues Guitar

The Big Book of Blues Guitar

The History, the Greats
—And How to Play

ANDREW LEO LOVATO

Terra Nova Books
Santa Fe, New Mexico

Library of Congress Control Number 2019948005
Distributed by SCB Distributors, (800) 729-6423

Terra Nova Books

The Big Book of Blues Guitar. Copyright © 2019 by Andrew Leo Lovato
All rights reserved
Printed in the United States of America

TerraNovaBooks.com
AndrewLeoLovato.com
TheBigBookOfBluesGuitar.com

ISBN 978-1-948749-41-1

*In memory of Wally Graham, who taught me the
fine points of soul surfing.*

Contents

Illustrations and Photos

Introduction

Man, I love the blues.
Boy, I love the guitar.
And I love it most when we put them both together!
And you? I'm guessing that if you're checking out this book and reading these lines, the blues guitar has a pretty powerful hold on you too. Likely, you've been touched as I have by the emotion, the depth, and the majesty of this truly American musical art form born deep in the Mississippi Delta.

Perhaps the only thing better than listening to the blues is playing the blues yourself and feeling the music come to life under your fingers. If that's where you're coming from—if you can feel the magic I'm talking about—then this book is for you.

I'm here to be your guide on the exciting journey into the world of blues guitar by helping you understand what it takes, build your skills, and express your own personal style in your music.

Some readers picking up this book will be beginners at playing the guitar but nevertheless, lovers of its sound and of the blues. Others with some basic guitar skills and practice under their belts may be interested in taking their playing to a higher level through the new techniques and exercises I will share. Perhaps you've been playing for a few years and feel like you're stuck repeating the same songs and riffs. My goal is to shake things up a little and get your playing going in new and more-creative directions.

Whatever your skill level and experience, this book will help bring a broader and deeper range to your music. We'll begin by talking about the development of basic blues guitar skills, with the Guitar Guide for Beginners chapter offering the key elements needed to master the fundamentals for those who may be just starting out.

For readers who can skip ahead, the book's more-advanced material will aid in taking your rhythm playing and solo techniques to the next level of blues progressions, grooves, and improvisation.

1

As with every great art form, there are an unlimited number of ways to dissect and approach the creative process involved in playing the blues, and I can't claim to cover every aspect of blues guitar in this book. Rather, I'm hoping to offer a starting point through which you can advance your own unique style and perhaps better understand the blues when you listen to the guitar greats we all admire.

Together, we are following in the path of the awe-inspiring legacy left by blues guitarists over the generations. As listening to and feeling its beat makes clear, there may never have been a more fortuitous marriage between an instrument and a music genre than that of the guitar and the blues.

Close your eyes and perhaps you can hear Eric Clapton's exquisitely crafted solo in, "Nobody Knows You When You're Down and Out," or the powerful, biting guitar of Albert King in his classic, "Blues Power." The joyous fingerpicking virtuosity of Mississippi John Hurt in "Candy Man" is incomparable, and Duane Allman's slide guitar on "At Fillmore East" transcends description. Stevie Ray Vaughan and Johnny Winter blister through the blues guitar with fire and passion. Or pick any track from the few recordings left for posterity by Robert Johnson to feel the real soul of the blues. And then there's B.B. King.

My own encounter with the blues is probably like that of many people smitten with this music. I was around thirteen when I checked out an album from the local library in Santa Fe, New Mexico, by a musician with the intriguing name of Howlin' Wolf. I had no idea what sort of music was contained in those grooves, but when I heard it for the first time, my world changed. The music coming from my speakers was different from anything I had ever encountered. The guttural, crackling voice and heavy-handed guitar playing conveyed energy and emotions that simultaneously frightened and attracted me.

Soon, I was carrying home stacks of albums from the library and scouring local record shops to find other creators of this strange and powerful music. It wasn't long before I came to know the work of artists like Charley Patton, Lightnin' Hopkins, John Lee Hooker, Muddy Waters, and Robert Johnson.

I convinced my father to buy a $30 Harmony steel string guitar of questionable quality. Nonetheless, I loved it. I spent all my free time after school tearing up my fingers trying to reproduce the string-bending techniques of my blues heroes.

Once you get the fever, I don't think you can ever recover. And I know that I'm not alone in this but instead I'm part of a global community joined by our love for this music born of pain and oppression. To be human is to feel the blues at one time or another, and to cry out to the world at the top of your lungs and from the bottom of your heart, "I've been down so long that it seems like up to me."

As you read on, I'll be talking about the history of the guitar and of the blues, and how the blues guitar—blessed by the great musicians who gave it their heart and soul—has evolved as a musical force shaping countless aspects of American culture.

The lessons in this book have been the basis of my thirty-plus years of teaching the guitar. Combined, they form the most direct method I know of for learning to play blues guitar and creating a rewarding and creative relationship with the guitar that will last a lifetime. You won't find much music theory in the book (though at times a little is unavoidable). My goal is to keep the learning process as accessible as possible for readers without much formal musical training.

Later in the book, I provide brief biographies of legendary guitarists who have shaped the blues, along with album picks of their best recordings. Although including all the worthy albums and great blues guitarists would be impossible, I hope it at least gives readers a start toward knowing and appreciating the legacy of blues guitar masters who have stretched the possibilities of their instrument to both entertain us and to stir our hearts and souls as well. I have also included a few personal guitar musings of my own—what this great music has meant to me over a life immersed in the guitar, the blues, and the wonderful joy they can bring together.

Long live the blues!

The Birth of the Guitar

Trying to figure out when and where the guitar was born is next to impossible. Historians and scholars haven't had much luck coming up with one specific place or moment in time when someone had an inspired eureka moment and came up with the creation we know as the guitar. The truth is that the guitar as we know it came into existence over centuries and went through all sorts of changes before morphing into the instrument we love today. Some researchers say the guitar got its start in Asia, some cite Africa, others Europe. No one agrees on the exact details, and it is unlikely that anyone ever will.

That's not to say there is a lack of intriguing clues. The ancient Hittites who lived about two thousand years ago in Anatolia (the Asian portion of Turkey) and northern Syria left behind some interesting artwork showing a musician playing what looks very similar to an early version of a guitar—a hollow, wooden, stringed instrument with a fretted neck.

Early versions of the guitar sprang up in ancient Greece, Rome, Egypt, and Persia. A classical Greek myth credits Hermes—who, in addition to his many other attributes, was the god of invention—with creating a guitar-like instrument from an unlucky tortoise by hollowing out its shell and adding cow-gut strings in an attempt to create divinely inspired music. Apollo, the Roman god of music, also was said to have experimented with creating an early version of the guitar using turtle shells and wooden bowls strung with gut strings.

The "cithara," a seven-stringed instrument from which the guitar got its name, was widely played at public events and religious festivals in Greece and Rome. Guitar historian Frederick Grunfeld speculated that perhaps the Roman Emperor Nero was not fiddling as Rome burned but instead was playing his cithara.

Myths aside, we can see the guitar as an offspring of other ancient instruments like the harp, lyre, and lute—and the sitar from India is another distant ancestor.

The Moors developed a four-stringed guitar-like instrument in the eighth century called the "oud," and the Vikings brought an instrument called the "lut," which could have been an early relative of the guitar, to other parts of Europe in medieval times.

The guitar's evolution into the instrument we know today began in Spain around the thirteenth century. The "guitarra moresca," or Moorish guitar, gained popularity and resembled the modern guitar with its rounded back, fingerboard, and sound holes in the body. This version of the early guitar spread to the New World and other parts of the globe through the voyages of the early Spanish explorers and settlers.

The lute was the stringed instrument of choice in other parts of Europe during this time, and may have evolved separately from the Spanish guitarra. The guitarra had four pairs of strings (called "courses") that were tuned to the same note, and the lute in Europe had eight pairs of strings (both similar in concept to a modern twelve-string guitar, which has six courses of strings). The large number of strings, and the fact that they needed to be made of dried animal intestines, made tuning difficult for aspiring musicians. Guitar scholar Joe Gioia quotes an early musician who commented that lutists "spent more time tuning than playing."

A four-course guitar was being used in French theater in the late 1400s, and guitars began to appear in England by the mid-1500s. In the 1600s, guitars were in fashion in the English court because the king, Charles II, was an aspiring guitarist.

The first guitar hero may have been an Italian named Francisco Corbetta who was renowned for his skill in both Italy and England. Corbetta inspired an appreciation for the guitar that began to take root in France, Spain, Italy, and other European countries. Because of the guitar's growing popularity in the 1500s and 1600s, a large body of music was composed for it across Europe.

After Spanish settlers, soldiers, and missionaries brought along their musical instruments on their ocean voyages to North, Central, and South America, Mexico City became a Spanish cultural hub where guitars were plentiful, and the equivalent of sheet music for the guitar could be acquired. As the Spanish ventured north, the guitar's influence and popularity spread to what are now New Mexico, California, and Texas.

At the same time, the guitar also was making its way into the territory that would become the United States via other avenues, such as English-made guitars brought across the Atlantic by colonial settlers. Black slaves from West Africa who had encountered guitar-like instruments through their association with the Moors and Portuguese created their own stringed instruments in America.

It was not long before several diverse versions of guitar-like music were spreading across the country, influenced by the cultures that were beginning to make up the social fabric of the forming nation. What is most remarkable about the popularity of the guitar in American history is the way it has been adapted to express and reflect the dreams, struggles, emotions, and character of the wide diversity of cultures that have made the U.S. their home.

Today, the guitar is the most popular musical instrument in the country, with an estimated 20 million in circulation. Every year, another million acoustic guitars and an additional million electric guitars are purchased in the U.S. More guitars are sold in this country than all other instruments combined. Truly, this six-string music box has struck a profoundly deep chord in the American collective psyche.

The Guitarists Who Gave Us the Blues

Perhaps no other musical style has historically influenced guitarists in America as much as the blues. Originally, black blues guitarists often made their own instruments from scrap wood, cigar boxes, and wire. But despite the primitive nature of their guitars, they transformed its possibilities and invented a new form of music that was so unique and expressive that it has endured as a central influence in modern popular music.

Early blues guitarists played their music as an expression of their struggles and poverty, honing their talents in obscurity with so little compensation that the guitar was referred to as the "starvation box."

The blues originated during the era of slavery in America. Workers in the fields would participate in field hollers and work songs as they labored. Often, these songs were characterized by call and response, vocal improvisation, and rhythmic chants. The notes and inflections of the songs were influenced by the music the singers had learned in their native lands or which had been passed down from those originally forced into slavery.

Many of the great blues guitarists and singers were descendants of slaves who lived in the Mississippi Delta region of the South in the early 1900s. Rural Delta blues masters included such legendary names as Robert Johnson, Muddy Waters, John Lee Hooker, Howlin' Wolf, and B.B. King.

Mississippi guitarist Robert Johnson is perhaps the most revered of the rural blues musicians. Legend has it that in a clandestine meeting with the devil at a discreet Delta crossroad, Johnson traded his soul in exchange for his talent. The complexity and intensity of his acoustic guitar style became a major influence on future generations of guitarists, although he recorded only twenty-nine songs in 1936 and '37 before his death at the age of twenty-seven.

A contemporary of Johnson's who also lived a brief but influential life was Blind Lemon Jefferson, who was known for a guitar technique that incorporated a wide range of other musical styles. He left behind over a hundred recordings before dying at the age of thirty-three.

A less-well-known but innovative blues trailblazer was Charley Patton, who has been referred to as the "Father of the Delta Blues." He incorporated the slide guitar technique, also known as bottleneck guitar, into the blues. Patton, who was of African-American and Native American heritage, used a variety of objects such as the neck of a glass bottle or the edge of a knife to slide over the strings of his guitar, which were tuned to an open chord.

Blues guitarist T-Bone Walker was a protégé of Blind Lemon Jefferson and learned his craft as a boy accompanying Jefferson through the streets of Dallas. Walker helped forge the transition from acoustic blues guitar to the advent of electric blues guitar in the late 1930s and '40s.

The guitarist who brought electric blues to the forefront was Muddy Waters early in the 1940s. He has been cited as a key influence on many rock and blues guitarists including B.B. King, the Rolling Stones, and Eric Clapton. Waters brought his electric blues guitar playing to Chicago in 1943 and defined what would come to be called the "Chicago Sound," which featured overloaded amplifiers creating a gritty distortion that would become an often-emulated guitar tone for rock and blues guitarists for decades to come. Classic examples of Muddy Waters' rough-edged guitar playing and growling blues vocals can be heard on two of his most popular hits, "Mannish Boy" and "I'm Your Hoochie Coochie Man."

Mississippi native B.B. King is perhaps the world's best-known blues guitarist and singer. His style was less raucous and more melodic than Muddy Waters'. King's career spanned over four decades, and he made more than fifty albums. His style of playing is deceptively simple, using tasteful bends and melodic runs. He toured extensively until his death in 2015, attracting new generations of fans who continued to be attracted to his style of the blues.

The rich history of blues guitar created by these masters and other great electric blues guitarists like Howlin' Wolf, Elmore James, and John Lee Hooker is constantly being discovered by new legions of players who continue to draw renewed inspiration from them.

Black blues guitarists were the wellspring for popular music in the U.S. during the last half of the twentieth century. The rock 'n' roll and rhythm and blues musical explosions that swept the country beginning in the

1950s were direct stepchildren of the blues. It is ironic that great blues guitarists like Muddy Waters, Robert Johnson, T-Bone Walker, and Howlin' Wolf were virtually ignored by the public until admiring white musicians acknowledged their debt to them.

To a significant degree, it was the British Invasion of the 1960s that led American audiences to "rediscover" the musical treasure that had remained undetected under their noses for decades. British rock bands such as the Rolling Stones, the Beatles, and the Animals proclaimed an almost-hero-like worship of these founding American blues musicians.

It is indisputable that the blues are the basis of rock music. Rock 'n' roll singing styles, guitar riffs, and chord progressions are all greatly indebted to the early blues giants. The list of blues apprentices who became rock stars in the U.S. and across the world is impressive—Janis Joplin, Jimi Hendrix, Led Zeppelin, the Allman Brothers, Stevie Ray Vaughan, Eric Clapton, and many, many others.

Elvis Presley was the first white performer to bring the energy and sensuality of the blues to a mass American audience. Backed by electric guitarist Scotty Moore and bassist Bill Black, Elvis exploded on the national musical scene in 1956 with "Heartbreak Hotel," quickly followed by other hits like "Don't Be Cruel," "Hound Dog," and "All Shook Up." He went on to become the face of rock 'n' roll and its biggest star, selling over a billion records worldwide.

Perhaps the first true rock 'n' roll guitar hero was Chuck Berry. He began recording in the 1950s and modeled his guitar-playing style after blues guitarist T-Bone Walker. Berry's dynamic stage appearance featured him sliding across the stage and doing his famous duck walk, with his guitar slung low.

British rock 'n' roll was rooted in black American electric blues. The more hard-edged British blues music originated in London and was influenced by American blues guitarists like Muddy Waters and Howlin' Wolf.

The Rolling Stones were part of this musical tradition, playing their own interpretations of the Chicago electric blues that they reverently admired, riffs and techniques copied by Rolling Stones guitarists Keith Richards and Brian Jones.

English guitarist Eric Clapton idolized blues legend Robert Johnson and dedicated himself to learning from American blues greats including Freddie King, Buddy Guy, and T-Bone Walker. Clapton's guitar was a powerful force with John Mayall's Bluesbreakers, the Yardbirds, and Cream, followed by a highly successful solo career.

The true personification of the blues was guitarist Jimi Hendrix, who used an arsenal of guitar sound effects like the wah-wah pedal, distortion, and screaming feedback. His electrifying stage presence borrowed heavily from blues guitarist T-Bone Walker with antics such as playing the guitar with his teeth and behind his back. Hendrix was a master at simultaneously incorporating lead and rhythm guitar parts into his playing in the tradition of Robert Johnson.

The late 1950s and early '60s ushered in a folk music revival in the U.S. and a resurgence of the popularity of the acoustic steel-string guitar. Artists like Pete Seeger, Doc Watson, Dave Van Ronk, and Big Bill Broonzy gained renewed popularity. Enthusiasts seeking to uncover the roots of folk music rediscovered previously obscure folk/blues guitarists and singers including Lead Belly, Lightnin' Hopkins, Mississippi John Hurt, and Son House.

The 1970s was a decade of earsplitting guitar amplification and arena rock shows. No band typified this more than Led Zeppelin, who combined the Chicago blues style guitar playing of Jimmy Page and Celtic folk music to create a supergroup that toured the U.S. frequently during the decade.

In more-recent years, Bonnie Raitt, an American singer-songwriter best known for her bottleneck slide guitar playing style, and Stevie Ray Vaughan, who fueled the blues revival of the 1980s with his accomplished guitar playing, have kept the blues front-and-center in the ears and hearts of music lovers across America and throughout the world.

Blues Guitar Basics

The 12-Bar Blues

Describing the musical form of the blues must begin with the basic structure of the 12-bar blues. Although there are many variations, this is the basis of the blues, and all blues songs, no matter how innovative or complex, branch off from this original 12-bar blues base.

Twelve bars refer to the number of measures within a blues song, which typically consist of four beats per measure. Thus, if a blues song's basic structure is twelve measures long and each measure has four beats, you can say that it follows the basic blues structure. This structure if often repeated within a blues song.

The next element that must conform in a basic blues song is a specific chord progression.

A chord is a combination of notes that are played together to produce a specific sound. Some chords are called major chords, and have a brighter, cheerier sound; others are minor chords, with a darker, sadder sound. What makes them sound different is the second note in the chord.

A C-major chord, for instance, consists of the notes C, E, and G, which are the first, third and fifth notes in the C major scale. On the other hand, a C-minor chord consists of C, E-flat, and G which are the first, third, and fifth notes in the C-minor scale.

Every key has its own family of chords, which are indicated by the numbers 1 through 7 heading the columns in the chart below. We call these "families" because the chords in each one share the same notes, and as a result, blend well together. They can be mixed in just about any sequence, and the results will sound good. Blues songs generally consist of 1-4-5 chords which create the signature sound of the blues. This means, for instance, as the chart shows, that a blues song in the key of C will use the chords of C major, F, and G (the first, fourth, and fifth in its family). And in the same way, a blues song in the key of F will use the chords F, B-flat, and C.

Note that in every key, Columns 1, 4, and 5 are all major chords, and Columns 2, 3, 6, and 7 are all minor chords. The chords in Column 7 (minor 7♭5) are not often used in the blues or other popular music forms, so we can ignore them for now.

Chord Progression Guide

1 (Key) Major	2 Minor	3 Minor	4 Major	5 Major or 7	6 Minor	7 Minor 7♭5
C	Dm	Em	F	G	Am	Bm7♭5
D♭	E♭m	Fm	G♭	A♭	B♭m	Cm7♭5
D	Em	F#m	G	A	Bm	C#m7♭5
E♭	Fm	Gm	A♭	B♭	Cm	Dm7♭5
E	F#m	G#m	A	B	C#m	D#m7♭5
F	Gm	Am	B♭	C	Dm	Em7♭5
G♭	A♭m	B♭m	C♭	D♭	E♭m	Fm7♭5
G	Am	Bm	C	D	Em	F#m7♭5
A♭	B♭m	Cm	D♭	E♭	Fm	Gm7♭5
A	Bm	C#m	D	E	F#m	G#m7♭5
B♭	Cm	Dm	E♭	F	Gm	Am7♭5
B	C#m	D#m	E	F#	G#m	A#m7♭5

Many songs use only those chords in a key's specific chord family, which surely helps simplify the mystery surrounding song construction. You might be surprised how many big hits and beloved classics achieve their success with this formula. Since most of them ignore the m7♭5 chord, this means that if you begin a song with a C chord, for instance, there are only five other chords that will likely follow in the rest of the song: Dm, Em, F, G, and Am. And as we've noted, in the case of the blues, this can be condensed even further since the basic 12-bar blues song uses only the 1-4-5 chords.

A well-known example of the 12-bar blues format is the song "Hound Dog," which Elvis Presley made into an international hit. It has been recorded over two hundred fifty times since Willie Mae "Big Mama" Thornton did it first on August 13, 1952.

Strum the song and change to the chord indicated when it appears above the lyrics to get a feel for a typical blues progression using the 1-4-5 chords—which means C, F, and G are the only chords you'll be using.

C
You ain't nothin' but a hound dog

Cryin' all the time
                 F
You ain't nothin' but a hound dog
             C
Cryin' all the time
        G   **F**   **C**
You ain't never caught a rabbit, and you ain't no friend of mine

Often, songs are played in different keys to accommodate the vocal range of the singer. For example, Elvis sang "Hound Dog" in the key of C, and Big Mama Thornton sang it in E♭.

If Hound Dog was played in the key of A instead of Elvis's C, the 1 chord would be A, the 4 chord D and the 5 chord E. If we chose the key of G, the 1 chord would be G, the 4 chord C, and the 5 chord D. The Chord Progression Guide tells you the 1-4-5 chords in any key simply by following the rows across.

In addition to the specific number of bars and the chords that are used, the typical blues song has certain notes, both the ones played by the guitar and those of the melody being sung. We'll use the key of C (the C-major scale) as the simplest example since it has no sharps or flats, and then we'll make a few changes to get the notes that best give us a blues sound.

First, instead of using all seven notes in the C major scale, we are going to use only the five of them (called a pentatonic scale) that are traditionally chosen for blues music. In this case, they're C-E-F-G-B.

Next, we will flat the second note in the C-major pentatonic scale to make it an Eb, and also flat the fifth note in the scale to make it a Bb. What results (C-E♭-F-G-B♭) is called a C blues scale. Flatting the second and fifth notes in the scale is what gives the song its distinctive sound and a blues feel.

A musician may choose to slide or bend some or all of these notes rather than play them in a direct fashion. (How to do this is discussed in the Guitar Guide for Beginners chapter.) This fluid approach also helps give the blues its distinctive and emotional character.

This next chart shows the notes that create a blues sound in every key: the first, the flatted third, the fourth, the fifth, and the flatted seventh—using the flat (♭) notation for ease of reading.

Blues Scale Formula in All Keys

1 (Key)	♭3	4	5	♭7
C	E♭	F	G	B♭
D♭	E	G♭	A♭	B
D	F	G	A	C
E♭	G♭	A♭	B♭	D♭
E	G	A	B	D
F	A♭	B♭	C	E♭
G♭	A	B	D♭	E
G	B♭	C	D	F
A♭	B	D♭	E♭	G♭
A	C	D	E	G
B♭	D♭	E♭	F	A♭
B	D	E	G♭	A

The final basic structure that is always common to 12-bar blues is lyrical rather than musical; it's the way repetitions are used: A line of lyrics is sung, then it's repeated, and after that, a different third line ends the verse.

In the example of "Hound Dog," we hear, "You ain't nothin' but a hound dog, cryin' all the time" sung twice and then followed by the verse's different last line: "You ain't never caught a rabbit, and you ain't no friend of mine."

Summing up, the basis of the blues consists of:
- The 12-bar measure form;
- The 1-4-5 chords in the key;
- The blues notes, that is the 1, ♭3, 4, 5, and ♭7 notes in a key;
- Bending pitches and sliding between notes; and
- A line of lyrics sung and repeated, with a third line concluding the verse.

With this as the foundation, an infinite number of variations can be created—the constant addition of new, diverse, and original elements that keep the blues vibrant and alive. The blues never stop changing and growing because of all the countless improvisational offshoots from the basic form that musicians keep creating.

The information in this chapter is a start, but in the final analysis, describing the blues in such a formulaic way seems terribly inadequate. The blues is so much more than song structure, designated notes, and a lyrical formula. What has connected it with the hearts of so many people over time is the way those notes can be used to express the unbridled emotion and yearning that is an inescapable part of the human condition. The blues can make you cry or laugh for joy, express the most profound hope-lessness, or reflect the wonder of human resilience. This magical music— born out of the struggles and suffering of the black Africans brought to America as slaves—has continued to evolve and transform itself under the loving guidance of blues musicians and fans covering every spectrum of the human family. The blues will never be neatly pigeonholed or even adequately described using mere words because of the power with which it reflects and expresses the boundless soul of people everywhere.

Finding the Right Notes to Jam: Blues Guitar Scales

A good method for learning to play blues guitar is to become familiar with some basic scale patterns. Then you can play these while other mu-sicians are laying down the chords, or between your own chords as you play the guitar. These scale patterns provide notes that create licks, or musical phrases, that fit inside blues songs.

To play these scales, hold your guitar pick between your thumb and first finger. Use alternating down and up strokes to improve your speed and agility.

Let's begin with the basic blues scale. We'll start with the F blues scale at the first fret of the guitar's neck, just like an F chord. Although you are beginning to learn the blues scale in the key of F, we will be covering the other keys as you progress in the book.

Basic Blues Guitar Scale

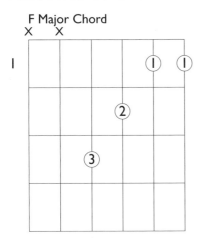

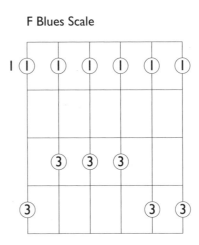

Each time you place your fingers as indicated, use your pick to play the notes, using alternating down and up strokes:

- Begin by placing your third finger on the fourth fret of the first string and playing this note.
- Next, place your first finger on the first fret of the first string, and play the note. Continue playing the notes as you move your fingers into the different positions.
- Place your third finger on the fourth fret of the second string.
- Place your first finger on the first fret of the second string.
- Place your third finger on the third fret of the third string.
- Place your first finger on the first fret of the third string.
- Place your third finger on the third fret of the fourth string.
- Place your first finger on the first fret of the fourth string.
- Place your third finger on the third fret of the fifth string.
- Place your first finger on the first fret of the fifth string.
- Place your third finger on the fourth fret of the sixth string.
- Place your first finger on the first fret of the sixth string.

You have just played the F blues scale from the first string to the sixth in descending tonal order. After doing this, play an F chord. You can hear how these notes sound in relation to the F chord; they sound rather bluesy. These are the basic notes in the F blues scale.

Practice this scale pattern until you can do it easily without looking at the illustration. At some point, try going in the opposite direction from the lowest note on the first fret of the sixth string to the highest note in the scale on the fourth fret of the first string.

Practice the scale in both directions bottom to top and top to bottom until you have it memorized in your fingers.

Once you've done this, you're off to a great start, but it still won't sound very musical. Then it's time to start making it more like the blues that accomplished guitarists play. The way to do this is by improvising within the scale. This means mixing up the notes and changing the rhythm.

Try playing the notes you've learned in a different order as you run through the F blues scale. Go up the scale for a couple of notes and then down two or three notes, or maybe hit the same note two or three times in a row. Play some notes quickly together and then hold other notes longer. Make your playing more unpredictable than simply going straight up or down the scale.

Great blues guitarists can create breathtaking solos using the same basic notes you've learned in this first blues scale. Listen to some accomplished blues guitarists to get a feel for how they play the notes in the blues scale. The great blues players like B.B. King, Albert King, and Eric Clapton can inspire us all with the feel and musicality inherent in the blues. Have fun and let your fingers wander. There is no wrong way to play the scale; it's up to your imagination and musical sensibilities.

One way to explore the sound and technique of playing the blues scales is to combine the chords with lead guitar—solos and embellishments played "over" (meaning in addition to) the basic chords, which can be played either by the soloist or another musician. You can do this by practicing with another guitarist and taking turns playing the chords (the 1-4-5 chords: F, B♭, and C in the key of F) and the F lead scale, so that each of you can provide the background chords and also experience playing lead blues guitar. In essence, this is what is referred to as "jamming."

Another possibility would be buying a recording of musicians playing blues background chords for you while you practice your blues scales and improvising. These are widely available online and are great for practicing, providing a professional backup band that's there only to accompany you. And the recordings also tell you the music's key to help you play along with it.

Blues Guitar Up and Down the Neck: The F Blues Scale in Different Positions

The F blues scale you have been working on is one of five F blues scales that cover the entire neck of the guitar in the key of F. By mastering the five scales illustrated in the key of F, you will be able to use the entire neck of the guitar as you improvise your blues lead guitar solos. This is because the blues scales in any key (such as F) becomes the blues scales in any other key simply by moving the same fingering to different frets. Being able to change from one key to another by moving your fingering elsewhere on the neck applies to the blues scale in any key.

For instance, these are the keys the F blues scale becomes when you move it up the neck:

Second fret—G♭	Sixth fret—B♭	Tenth fret—D
Third fret—G	Seventh fret—B	Eleventh fret—E♭
Fourth fret—A♭	Eighth fret—C	Twelfth fret—E
Fifth fret—A	Ninth fret—D♭	

Once you are able to play the blues scales in the key of F, later chapters will guide you in transposing these scales to other keys.

When your playing merges together the scales shown below, you will remain in the same key repeating the same five blues notes (such as F, Ab, Bb, Eb, and C if you're in the key of F) continually up and down the neck. Once you become fluent in going from one scale to another, you will be able to seamlessly play the notes up and down the neck, gliding from one scale to another or skipping scales and jumping smoothly from the lower part of the neck to a higher position.

In a sense, the blues scales "lock" into each other as the scales above and below each one overlap to share the same notes.

When you see experienced lead guitarists playing all over the neck with their eyes closed and seemingly always hitting the right notes as if by magic, it is because they have practiced these scales so many times that switching from one to another is second nature for them. Rather than having separate scales, their neck has become one large scale. When you get to this point, you can focus on sound and creativity and really begin having fun. But before you reach this stage, you will have to put in a lot of hard work memorizing and practicing these scales.

Become familiar with the blues scales. In the next section, you will learn to find the right fret locations to play them to match specific keys.

F Blues Scales

F Blues Root Chord

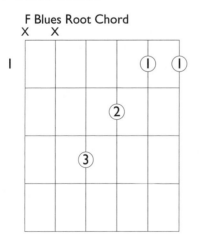
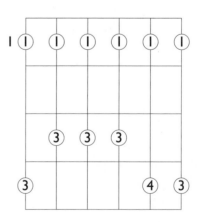

F Blues Scales (continued)

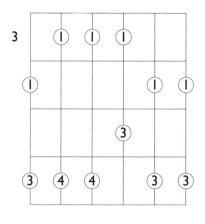

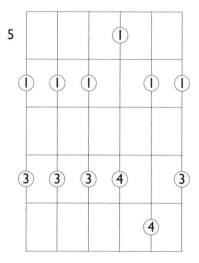

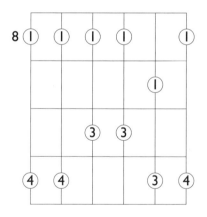

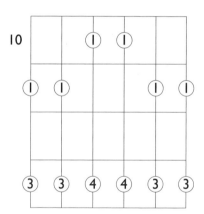

Got to Be Versatile, Man:
Playing the Blues Scale in Different Keys

Typically, blues songs do not change keys. They will generally stay exclusively in the key they begin in, and this is usually the song's first chord. This means that most of the time, a blues scale will correspond to the song's first chord and can be played over all other chords in the song as well. You do not change to a different blues scale every time you change chords, since the chords are usually in the same key. Instead, sticking for the entire song with blues scales that are in the same key as the first chord is a good rule of thumb in most cases.

For example, if you were playing a blues song that started with an F chord and changed to a B♭ chord and a C chord, you would play the F blues scale throughout the entire song even over the B♭ and C chords, because the B♭ is the 4 and the C chord is the 5 in the key of F.

To know where on the neck to play the blues scale, you will slide the F chord up the neck until it matches the first chord of the song you are playing. Then you should line up the basic F blues scale with this. Notice that the fret you place your first finger on in your basic blues scale will always be the same fret that your first finger goes on for the F major chord shape when you move it up the neck.

For example, if a blues song starts with an A chord, you will slide the F major chord up the neck to the fifth fret to make it an A chord since you know that:

First fret—F
Second fret—G♭
Third fret—G
Fourth fret—A♭
Fifth fret—A

Knowing that the F chord played on the fifth fret is an A chord, you can match up the blues scale to the chord. This means you will repeat the same blues scale pattern that you learned beginning with the first-fret F position but will play it four frets higher on the neck to play an A blues scale.

To play blues in the key of G, you follow the same process beginning on the third fret. Blues in B begins on the seventh fret, blues in C on the eighth fret, blues in D on the tenth fret, and so on.

Remember that the first chord in the song is usually the key you stay on all through it. For example, if a song starts with a G chord (two frets higher than an F-major chord), play a G blues scale (two frets higher than an F blues scale) through the entire song even if the chords change.

Three Essential Techniques for Playing Blues: The Bend, Hammer-On, and Slide

Bending strings is essential in playing blues lead guitar. It adds emotion and passion to the notes. Most bending is done on the first and second strings, but the technique can be used on the other strings as well.

To bend a string, you should push up on it against the neck of the guitar, which stretches it to produce a higher pitch. Bending is often done on the notes hit by the third finger in the blues scales, although other fingers are often used as well.

Try bending the first string on the fourth fret of the F blues scale. Push up on the string with the third finger at that fret to stretch it and raise the note. Now try doing the same thing on the fourth fret of the second string. This may hurt at first, but your fingers will toughen up as you work on it.

The hammer-on technique requires you to hold down a note on a fret as you come down hard on a higher fret with another finger to produce a second note. Here is an example using the F blues scale:

Place your first finger on the first fret of the third string. Hit this note with your pick and then come down hard and quickly with your third finger on the third fret of the third string while still holding the first fret down. If you do this smoothly and firmly, you should produce a second note when your finger comes down on the third fret. If done correctly, you will produce two notes with only one pick stroke. This technique is called the hammer-on.

Try this on the first and third frets of the F blues scale on the third, fourth, and fifth strings.

The slide is like the hammer-on in concept except that you slide from one note to another rather than coming down hard with a second finger.

Using the F blues scale, place your third finger on the first fret of the third string. When you hit this note, slide your finger up to the third fret while holding down on the string to produce a second note. You will produce two notes by sliding from the first fret up to the third fret.

Try this at the first and third frets of the F blues scale on the third, fourth, and fifth strings.

Using these three techniques when playing the blues scales will make your scale sound more like blues guitar playing and give your lead improvisation a more-authentic feel and sound.

The Chords That Make the Blues Sound Like the Blues: 7th Chords

Playing 7th chords is essential in creating the blues sound you want. These are made by adding the flatted seventh note in a scale to a major chord. Seventh chords are the heart and soul of the sound that we call the blues. By mastering the following 7th chords in different keys, you will be able to lay down the foundation for many classic blues songs. Illustrated below are the most useful and best-sounding F7 chord variations. You can create other 7th chords by moving them up or down the guitar neck. To create new chords, follow the notes in order as you did before with the blues scale.

Illustrated are five F7 chords on the neck of the guitar. Going up one fret for each of the F7 chords will make them a Gb7 chord, up one more fret, an G7 chord and so on. Going one fret down from the F7 chords would make them E7 chords, down another fret would turn them into Eb7 chords and so on.

F7 Chords

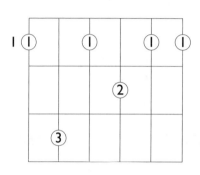

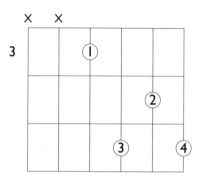

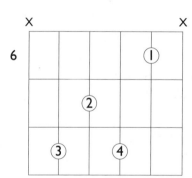

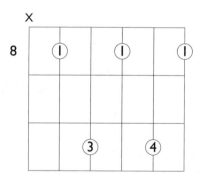

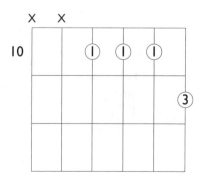

Putting It All Together:
Combining Blues Scales and 7th Chords

Each of the five blues scales has a complementary 7th chord that is easier to access than the other 7th chords because it's nearby. The ability to combine the five blues scales we've discussed with their complementary 7th chords will make your blues guitar playing more interesting and creative. Being able to switch smoothly from scales to chords at similar positions on the guitar neck will let you transition from chords to scales without having to jump up and down on the neck.

The following chart shows the five blues scales in the key of F with their complementary F7 chords. Practice playing and switching between the scales and the accompanying 7th chords until you can do it by memory. When you become comfortable doing this, you will be able to combine blues scales and 7th chords in a more-natural way.

F Blues Scale and F7 Chords

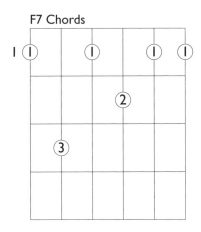

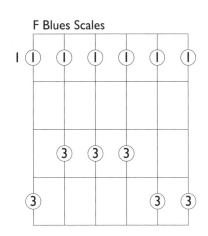

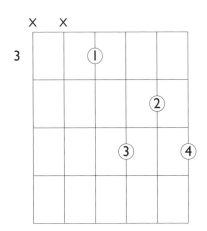

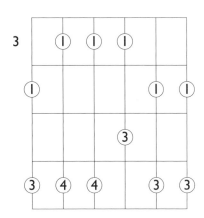

F Blues Scale and F7 Chords (continued)

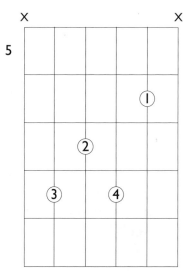

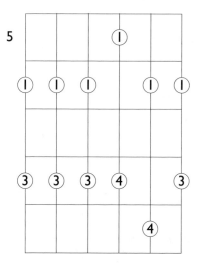

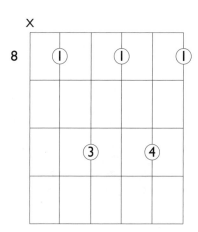

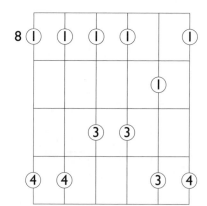

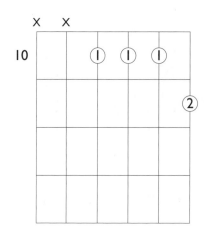

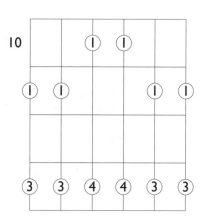

When you become familiar with doing this in the key of F, try the same thing in other keys by moving the scales and chords up and down the frets, playing in the different keys by following the sequence of notes along the neck of the guitar.

Finding the Lost Blues Chord: The 9th Chord

When you are playing a 7th chord in a blues song, you can create an interesting and appealing effect in the style of guitarists like Stevie Ray Vaughan by adding a 9th chord. For example, if you are playing a blues song in C, the standard 1-4-5 chord progression would be C-F-G, or—depending on what sound you want—any of those could be a 7th (C-F7-G, for instance), or they all could be (C7-F7-G7). You also can also substitute a 9th chord rather than a 7th chord for any of the 1-4-5 chords (C-F9-G, for instance, or C, F9, G7 if you wanted).

Experiment substituting the 9th for chords that you play in various places. I think you will like what you hear.

Each 9th chord starts at a specific fret, as shown below. You can create any 9th chords by following the standard note sequence one fret at a time. The 9th chords illustrated are B9 chords fingered beginning on the first fret.

First fret—B9	Fifth fret—E♭9	Ninth fret—G9
Second fret—C9	Sixth fret—E9	Tenth fret—A♭9
Third fret—D♭9	Seventh fret—F9	Eleventh fret—A9
Fourth fret—D9	Eighth fret—G♭9	Twelfth fret—B♭9

B9 Chords

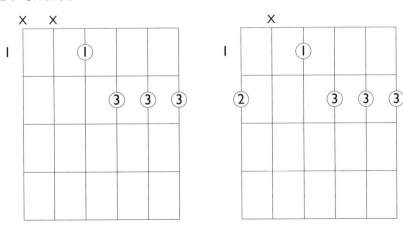

Beyond the Basic Blues

Playing Country Blues: The Folk/Country Scales

A quick and easy way of thinking of the folk/country scales is to realize that they're identical to the blues scales in shape and fingering. The only difference is that you play the folk/country scales three frets lower on your guitar neck than you would play the blues scales.

For example, if you are playing the following blues scale in the key of C, it would be on the eighth fret. When you play the identical scale on the fifth fret, it is the folk/country scale in the key of C.

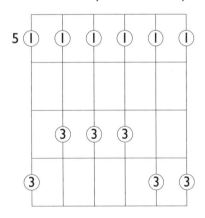

Blues Scale in the Key of C   Folk/Country Scale in the Key of C

We noted earlier that the blues scale is called the "minor pentatonic scale." In similar music terminology, the folk/country scale is the "major pentatonic scale." They are both called pentatonic scales because they consist of five notes. The blues scale is a minor pentatonic in which the second and fifth notes are flatted. In the folk/country, or major pentatonic scale, none of the five notes is altered.

You can combine these two scales and go from one to the other as you improvise, getting a very nice sound that might be referred to as "country-blues." The folk/country scale is often used in this way by blues players.

To play this scale, use the same method of connecting the scale to the F-shaped chord as it is moved up and down the neck. And the techniques of bending, hammer-on, and sliding can be used with the folk/country scale just as successfully as with the blues scale.

As shown below, the folk/country scale formed around a major-shaped chord played on the fifth fret will produce an A chord and an A folk/country scale.

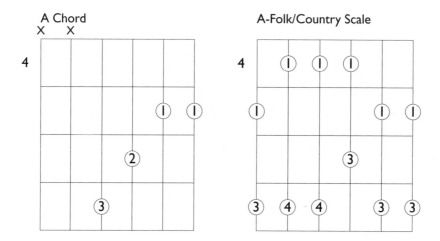

Notice that the folk/country scale illustrated above is the same as one of the blues scales you have been practicing. The five folk/country scales are the same finger patterns that you learned with the blues scales, and also merge with each other in the same way as the blues scales.

The same basic principles apply for the folk/country scale as with the blues scale. Simply running through the scale from top to bottom is not going to sound like folk or country. You need to begin improvising with the scale. This means mixing up the notes and changing their rhythm.

Listening to some of the great players like Doc Watson and Chet Atkins will give you a sense of how to play the notes in this scale, as well as inspire in you the feel and musicality inherent in country, folk, and bluegrass. Again, as with the blues scale, have fun and let your fingers wander. There is no wrong way to play the scale; it is up to your imagination and musical sensibilities.

Blues with a Santana Flavor: Minor 7th Scales

Minor 7th scales give you finger patterns you can use in all five positions on the neck to create a variety of very creative lead guitar possibilities by positioning the scales on different frets in relation to the key you are in and the chords you are playing.

For example, minor 7th scales can be substituted for blues scales to give a different flavor to your playing, since the blues scale is contained within the minor 7th scale. Carlos Santana's playing is a great example of this. You can think of the minor 7th scale as a blues scale with two notes added or a major scale with the 3rd and 7th notes flatted. Try rotating between the blues and minor 7th scales when playing lead guitar. The minor 7th scale will share the same key as the blues scale within it, which is next to it in the illustration below.

Blues Scales   **Minor 7th Scales**

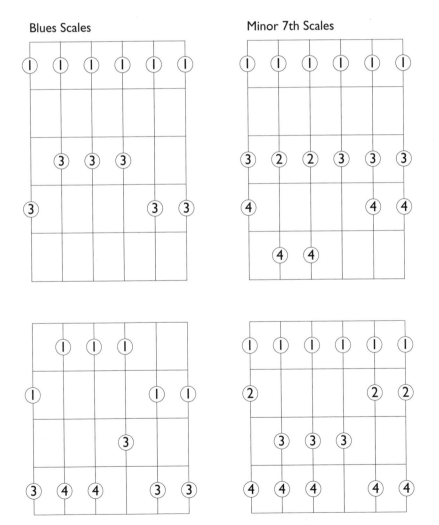

Blues Scales continued

Minor 7th Scales continued

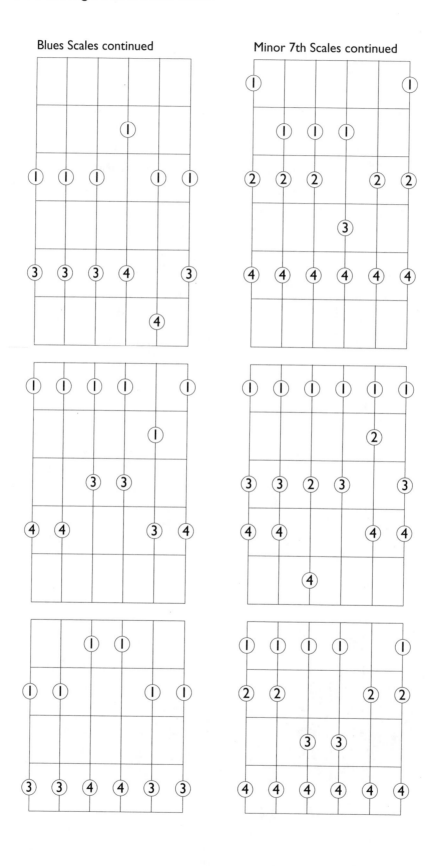

Exotic Blues Colorings: Modal Playing

Stepping outside the traditional blues notes when improvising a blues solo can create some very interesting effects. A great example of this is the masterpiece album by Miles Davis, *Kind of Blue*. In it, he gave his improvisation a unique feel and texture by superimposing over traditional blues chord structures a mode or coloring consisting of patterns of notes that they do not usually contain.

A number of blues guitarists have also used the idea of this type of modal playing to embellish their blues and "step outside the box." Jimi Hendrix and Carlos Santana are great examples of performers who have added notes outside the basic blues scale to create their signature sounds.

The illustrations below incorporate some interesting modes that can be mixed with the basic blues scale to add new melodic possibilities. Try weaving these around your blues scales from time to time to create new sounds.

The modal scales, in the illustration are superimposed around an A chord on the fifth fret. If you are playing blues in the key of A, you can use this guide to help find the right scales to play in different modes.

The varied scales making up these modes were inspired by the ancient Greeks (as their names show) and have been part of Western music since the Middle Ages. They are identical in pattern structure to the minor 7th scales shown earlier but are placed on different frets. Refer to the scale placed next to each A chord and add the scales above and below it, as you did with the minor 7th scales in the preceding chapter, to play up and down the neck.

Modal Scales in Relation to A Major Chord

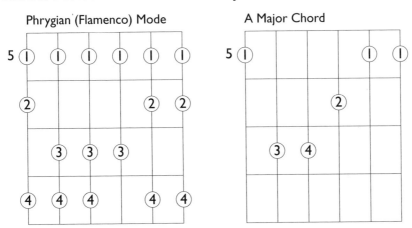

Modal Scales in Relation to A Major Chord (continued)

A Major Chord

Mixolydian (Jazz) Mode

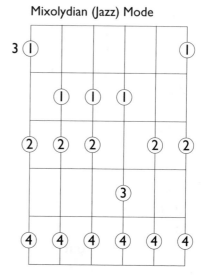

A Major Chord

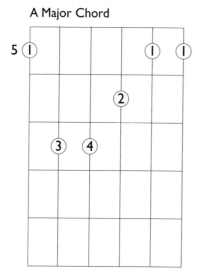

Dorian (Minor 7th) Mode

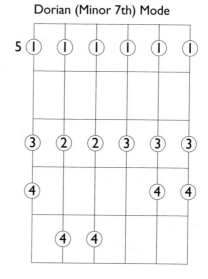

A Major Chord

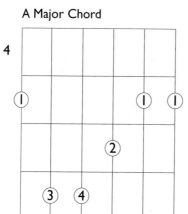

Ionian (Major) Mode

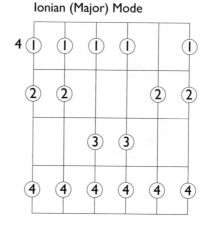

Roll Over Chuck Berry: Blues Scale Double-Stops

Hitting two notes in a blues scale at the same time is referred to as playing double-stops. This technique, in which the guitarist also hits another accessible note in the same scale, creates an interesting contrast to single-note playing, and is used in many musical styles.

For example, using double-stops in the blues scale is a common technique that has been used by blues guitarists and rock 'n' rollers alike. Chuck Berry's guitar riffs are good examples of this technique. Try incorporating these double-stop examples in the blues scales in the illustration to supplement your single-note playing.

Selected Blues Scale Double-Stops

Blues Scale

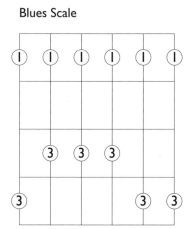

Blues Double-Stops

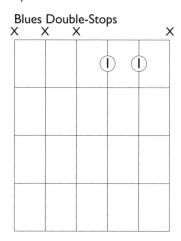

Blues Double-Stops

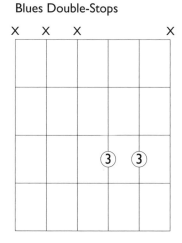

Blues Double-Stops

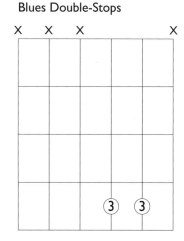

Cool Blues Jazz Stylings: Minor 7th Arpeggios

When playing the minor 7th scale patterns, guitarists often get into the rut of playing the notes in ascending or descending order, which can lead to predictable riffs and unimaginative playing. One way to break this up is with scale arpeggios in which you play every other note in the scale. Practicing arpeggios is a great way to make your lead guitar playing sound more interesting and more musical. You can skip the notes with the x's, and then play the scale again skipping the ones without x's.

Minor 7 Arpeggio Patterns

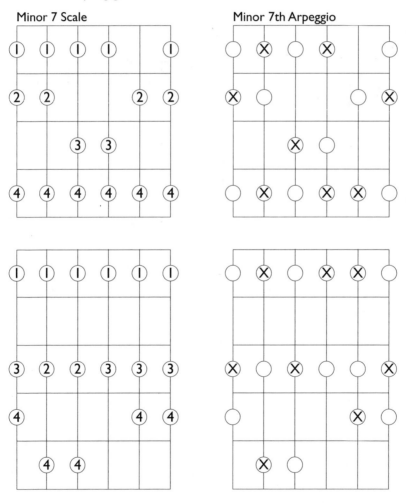

Minor 7 Arpeggio Patterns (continued)

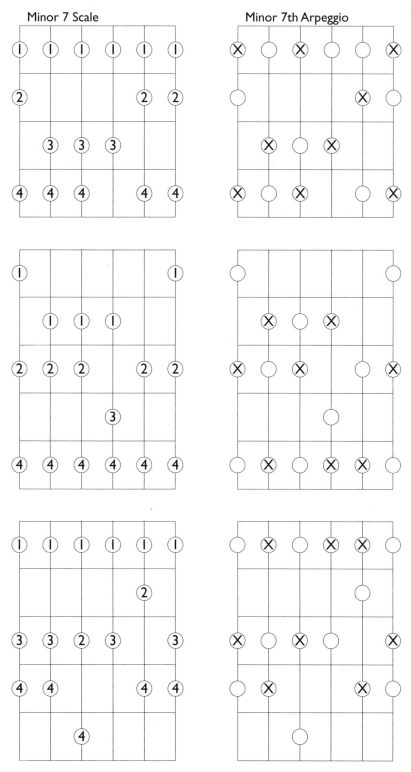

Minor 7 Scale   Minor 7th Arpeggio

Blues Passing Notes

Mastering the blues scales is key to discovering the notes that can be used when playing a blues guitar solo or adding embellishments within a song.

The following scales are identical to the blues scales in the key of F that were shown earlier in the book but with the addition of a "passing note."

This refers to a note in the blues scale that is not emphasized or lingered on but rather is used to transition to another note below or above it in the scale. Its presence adds a distinct and colorful flavor to lead guitar playing, making it an invaluable addition to any blues guitar player's repertoire.

The passing note that is illustrated is created by taking the fourth note (Bb) in the key of F (F-G-A-Bb-C-D-E) and raising it one fret to make a B note (while also keeping the original Bb note)—the fourth note in a scale being the one blues players use most often for this purpose. The blues scale in the key of F then becomes F-Ab-Bb-C-Eb + the B passing note.

I have added the most convenient passing notes to the scales below for you to experiment with. I think you will find the results quite pleasing. You can apply these passing notes to blues in all keys by following the same scale patterns shown below.

F Blues Scales with Additional B or #4 Passing Notes

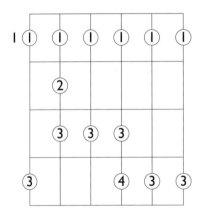 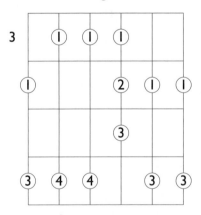

F Blues Scales with Additional B or #4 Passing Notes (continued)

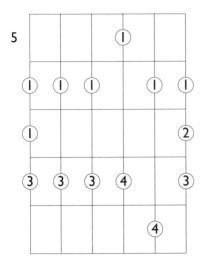

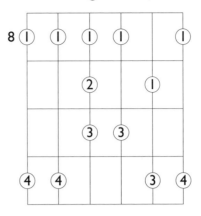

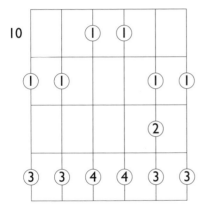

Fingerpicking and Slide Blues Guitar Tunings: Open Tunings

An "open tuning" is one in which the open strings are tuned to form a chord when they are strummed. The standard guitar tuning of E-A-D-G-B-E can be altered to produce some very interesting variations. One common method of open tuning is to tune the strings to a chord that lets a guitarist fingerpick and play embellishments without having to hold down a chord at all times. This is used by many guitarists who play blues slide guitar.

This technique has often been used by blues and folk guitarists to develop a unique picking style that creates an easier way to combine a melody line with the chords simultaneously. The blues guitar of Mississippi John Hurt is a good example of this type of playing.

Another example of a song that uses an open tuning is "Honky Tonk Women" by the Rolling Stones. It is played with the open strings tuned to a G chord, which gives the song a sliding, bluesy feel that can't be achieved in any other way.

D, G and C are the most common chords used for open tunings.

Open Tunings

D Open Tuning

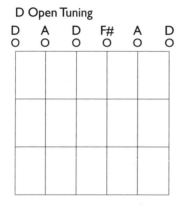

For D open tuning, the tunings are:
Sixth string—D
Fifth string—A
Fourth string—D
Third string—F#
Second string—A
First string—D

G Open Tuning

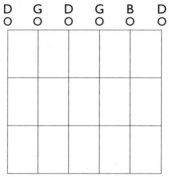

For G open tuning:
Sixth string—D
Fifth string—G
Fourth string—D
Third string—G
Second string—B
First string—D

C Open Tuning

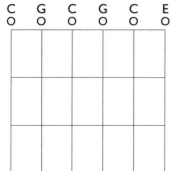

For C open tuning:
Sixth string—C
Fifth string—G
Fourth string—C
Third string—G
Second string—C
First string—E

Try these open tunings and have some fun. One challenge will be that you can't use the same chord shapes you are familiar with in regular tuning. Illustrated below are some basic I-4-5 chords in open D, G, and C tunings to get you started.

Open D Tunings—D, G, A Chords

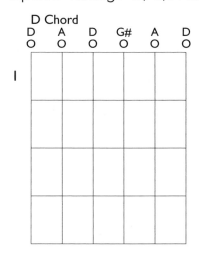

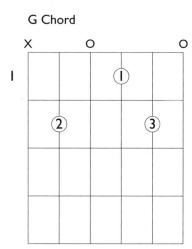

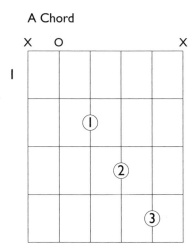

Open G Tunings—G, C, D Chords

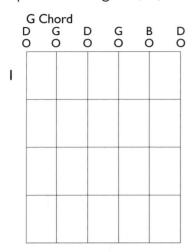

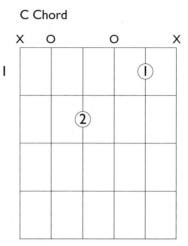

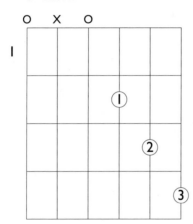

Open C Tunings—C, F, G Chords

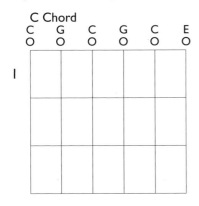

C Chord

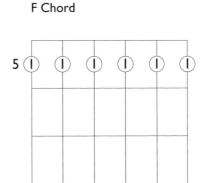

F Chord

G Chord

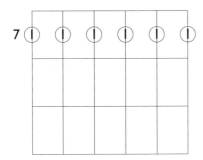

Note that with the open C chords, you are using your first finger to slide the entire open C chord up to the fifth fret to create an F chord and moving up to the seventh fret to create the G chord.

A Couple of Blues Chord Riffs You've Heard Before: Laying Down the Groove

The following are a couple of defining blues riffs used by many guitar players over the years. I'm sure you've heard them often before, and I think you'll enjoy experimenting with them in your own playing.

For each of the following three chords (A7-D-E), you will barre across all six strings with your first finger. The example shown of a 1-4-5 blues chord progression is in the key of A, requiring that you barre on the fifth and seventh frets.

On the A7 chord, you alternate on every beat between the seventh and ninth frets on the fifth string, using your third and fourth fingers.

On the D chord, you alternate between the seventh and ninth frets on the fourth string, using your third and fourth fingers.

On the E chord, you alternate between the ninth and eleventh frets on the fourth string, using your third and fourth fingers.

The versions of the D and E chords in the diagram are used for this riff to make it easier to play.

In a standard 12-bar blues song, you would play the A7 for bars 1-4, D for bars 5-6, A7 for bars 7-8, E for bar 9, D for bar 10, and A7 for bars 11-12.

Blues Chord Riff 1

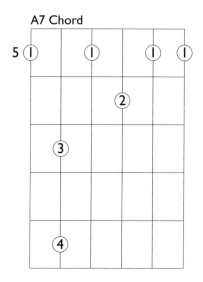

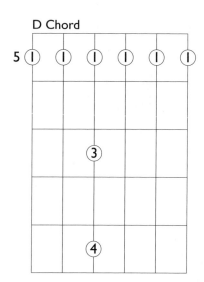

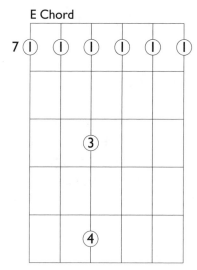

The following blues chord riff is called a turnaround because it creates a transition between the end of a 12-bar blues pattern and the beginning of a new 12-bar pattern. This turnaround will be played on bars 11-12 at the end of a 12-bar blues pattern.

Blues Chord Riff 2

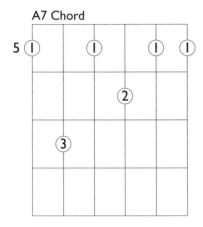

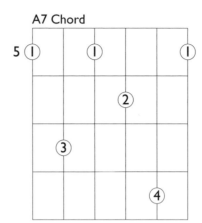

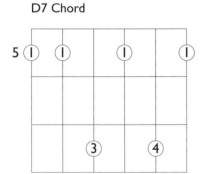

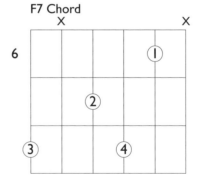

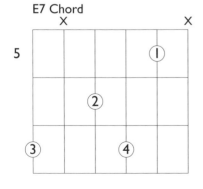

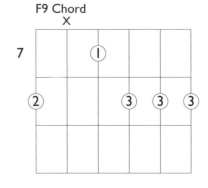

Blues Chord Riff 2 (continued)

E9 Chord

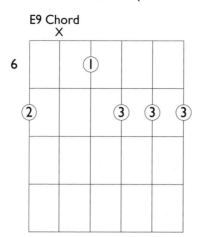

Legends of the Blues Guitar

Duane Allman   November 20, 1946–October 29, 1971

Duane Allman is known for his blues slide guitar playing and his inventive guitar solos with the Allman Brothers Band, which he formed with his brother, Greg, in 1969.

His blues guitar skills made him a sought-after session musician as well, and he brought his unique style to recordings by artists including Aretha Franklin, Wilson Pickett, and Boz Scaggs. Allman's most famous guest appearance was on the 1970 album *Layla and Other Assorted Love Songs*, by Eric Clapton's Derek and the Dominos.

He helped to establish the genre known as "Southern rock" during his short career. Allman was killed in a motorcycle crash shortly after the release and initial success of At Fillmore East.

Album pick: *Allman Brothers Band At Fillmore East*, Capricorn, 1997. Recorded in 1971, this album displays Duane Allman at the top of his game. Trading licks with Dickie Betts, he stretched his blues improvisational skills to the limit. Many modern blues guitarists have expanded their chops listening to this album. It's a must-have for electric blues guitar lovers.

Chuck Berry   October 18, 1926–March 18, 2017

It may seem odd to include Chuck Berry in a list of legendary blues guitarists but he's the man who took the blues and made it rock 'n' roll. Songs such as "Maybelline" (1955), "Roll Over Beethoven" (1956), "Rock and Roll Music" (1957), and "Johnny B. Goode" (1958) are firmly based in the blues stylistically, but Berry added a faster, stronger beat, and they became rock 'n' roll standards. He was one of the first to incorporate guitar solos into rock 'n' roll. His distinctive style of playing was upbeat, and his licks have become the training ground for many guitarists who have cited him as a major influence, including the Beatles and the Rolling Stones.

Album pick: *The Great Twenty-Eight*, Chess Records, 1982. This set of his hits leaves no doubt that Chuck Berry is the man who made the blues into rock 'n' roll.

Michael Bloomfield   July 28, 1943–February 15, 1981

Mike Bloomfield was renowned for his blues guitar skills beginning in the 1960s. He was a student of several of the blues legends as he honed his skills, including Sleepy John Estes, Muddy Waters, and Howlin' Wolf. Bloomfield was the featured guitarist for the Paul Butterfield Blues Band beginning in 1965, and also played in the Electric Flag group before pursuing a solo career.

He preferred a clean sound with reverb and vibrato as opposed to the distorted guitar sound of the 1960s. Bloomfield's use of chromatic and modal playing was unique among his peers. He has influenced the style of many modern guitarists including Robben Ford, John Scofield, and Eric Johnson.

Album pick: *The Paul Butterfield Blues Band: East/West*, 1966/2008, Electra Records. It can be argued that Bloomfield's best work came as a member of the bands he was in rather than as a soloist. In this album, he burns blues solos and adds a twist of modal playing to keep things interesting.

Joe Bonamassa   May 8, 1977

Joe Bonamassa began his blues career early, opening for B.B. King when he was twelve years old. He has recorded and toured extensively over his career, reaching No. 1 in the Billboard Blues charts many times. He has played with many contemporary blues guitar greats including Eric Clapton, Buddy Guy, and Derek Trucks.

Bonamassa runs a nonprofit organization called the Keeping the Blues Alive Foundation which funds scholarships and promotes music education resources. He is also known for his extensive collection of vintage guitars. Over a million fans subscribe to his newsletter.

Album pick: *Dust Bowl*, J&R Adventures, 2011. Bonamassa conjures up hot guitar blues/rock riffs and solos that are showcased in his stellar production and song arrangements. An album that shows aspiring blues guitarists what they can reach for.

Roy Buchanan   September 23, 1939–August 14, 1988

Roy Buchanan was a blues guitarist who is remembered for the sound of his Fender Telecaster, which he called "Nancy." Although he remained relatively unknown to the wider public, he was admired by many blues lovers for his guitar technique. Buchanan used a number of picking and harmonic effects to create his unique sound.

He earned a degree of national notice in 1971 through an hour-long PBS television documentary, "Introducing Roy Buchanan." He has sometimes been referred to as "the best unknown guitarist in the world." At one point, it was rumored that he had been invited to join the Rolling Stones and turned it down, which gave him his second nickname as "the man who turned down the Stones." He recorded several albums as both a sideman and a solo artist, including five for Polydor Records in the 1970s.

Album pick: *Roy Buchanan*, Polydor, 1972. There is a reason many blues guitar players cite this album as inspirational. Buchanan's emotion and technique on his Telecaster make the blues come alive.

Eric Clapton March 30, 1945

Eric Clapton is deservedly nicknamed "Slowhand" because of his speed and agility on the guitar. He is probably the most influential blues guitarist to emerge in the 1960s, and a towering figure for those who grew up in the baby-boom era. During the mid-'60s, graffiti would appear in England proclaiming, "Clapton is God." He has been influenced by Chicago blues greats like Buddy Guy, B.B. King, and Freddie King but often cites blues legend Robert Johnson as his main inspiration. His guitar work with The Yardbirds, John Mayall and the Bluesbreakers, Cream, and Derek and the Dominos, as well as his solo work, has made him a legend in his own right. Clapton's blues playing on acoustic guitar in addition to his electric guitar work highlights his versatility and love for the blues.

Album pick: *John Mayall and the Bluesbreakers with Eric Clapton*, Polygram Records, 1990. This album features early Clapton at his best, riffing with his Gibson Les Paul. And—because there's only one Clapton—here's a second album pick: *Derek and the Dominos: Layla and Other Assorted Love Songs*, Polydor, Anniversary Deluxe Edition, Remastered, 2011. This is considered by many to be the highlight of Clapton's recording career. The interplay of Clapton's and Duane Allman's blues guitar playing makes this album a modern standard.

Robert Cray August 1, 1953

Robert Cray forged a successful career after getting the blues bug as a young man seeing greats such as Albert Collins, Freddie King, and Muddy Waters.

He has performed and recorded with blues legends such as Eric Clapton, John Lee Hooker, and the man he cites as his main influence, Albert Collins. Fender, whose Stratocaster and Telecaster guitars have been played by Cray for much of his career, has released two Signature Stratocasters in his name. In 2006 and '07, he did a world tour with Eric Clapton.

Album pick: *Strong Persuader,* Mercury Records, 1986. Released to critical acclaim, this album combines Cray's compelling guitar playing with strong arrangements and finely crafted songwriting.

Reverend Gary Davis   April 30, 1896–May 5, 1972

Reverend Gary Davis was a blues and gospel singer whose fingerpicking guitar style influenced many other artists. Born in Laurens, South Carolina, he became blind as an infant. Davis took to the guitar and soon was playing gospel, ragtime, and blues tunes. He began recording his blues songs in 1935 but gave up the blues for gospel music after becoming a Baptist minister in 1937.

As with other blues guitarists of his time, the folk revival of the 1960s gave his career new life, and his songs were covered by artists such as Peter, Paul and Mary, the Grateful Dead, and Bob Dylan.

Album pick: *Pure Religion & Bad Company,* Smithsonian Folkways Recordings, 1991. Recorded in 1957, Davis's unique blues guitar style of picking and strumming, along with his "talking blues" and singing, capture an era when the blues and religion were compatible partners. The instrumental blues cuts are great as well.

Peter Green   October 29, 1946

Green is a British blues rock guitarist and the founder of Fleetwood Mac. He was a major force in the British blues movement. B.B. King and Eric Clapton are among the blues guitarists who have sung his praises, and music critics have ranked him highly as an accomplished guitarist with a unique tone and vibrato style.

Before founding Fleetwood Mac, Green was the lead guitarist for John Mayall's Bluesbreakers, replacing Clapton. Other career highlights included writing Santana's great "Black Magic Woman"; recording the guitar instrumental "Albatross," which was a No. 1 hit in Britain; and playing on the album *Blues Jam in Chicago* alongside blues greats Otis Spann, Willie Dixon, and Buddy Guy.

Album pick: *Peter Green & the Original Fleetwood Mac: Alone with the Blues,* Metro Select, 2015. Green was admired as a blues guitar player by many of his contemporaries in the 1960s, but mental health issues unfortunately robbed him of much potential. This collection showcases the originality of his blues guitar technique.

Buddy Guy July 30, 1936

Buddy Guy's blues guitar playing is heavily influenced by Muddy Waters, and he in turn has influenced such contemporary blues guitarists as Eric Clapton, Jimi Hendrix, Jimmy Page, Keith Richards, and Stevie Ray Vaughan.

Guy was a house guitarist at Chess Records alongside Muddy Waters during the 1960s, before he came into prominence in the 1980s and '90s. Much of his best work was in collaboration with harmonica player Junior Wells.

Guy's guitar playing is rooted in the Chicago blues style, but he has expanded this influence to create a unique style of his own which dabbles in a variety of genres, stretching the limits of blues.

Buddy Guy is also one of the few bluesmen who have chronicled their lives in books. In 1999, he wrote the book *Damn Right I've Got the Blues*. His autobiography, *When I Left Home: My Story*, was published in 2012.

Album pick: *Damn Right, I've Got the Blues*, Silvertone, 1991. Buddy Guy's comeback album after a long hiatus from the recording studio proved that he was still a force to be reckoned with. With guest help from the likes of Eric Clapton, Jeff Beck, and Mark Knopfler, the album won a Grammy in 1992.

Jimi Hendrix November 27, 1942–September 18, 1970

For all his experimentation musically and as a performer, Jimi Hendrix was, in essence, a blues guitarist. Behind all the sound effects and psychedelia is a solid blues foundation. Hendrix was voted No. 1 in Rolling Stone magazine's list of the hundred greatest guitarists of all time.

His musical odyssey began in 1957 when he found a one-string ukulele in the trash. Hendrix's brief stint in the Army was marked by harassment for playing the guitar too much. He was influenced by Muddy Waters, Howlin' Wolf, and B.B. King.

Hendrix formed his own band, the Jimi Hendrix Experience, in England in 1966 and became a guitar phenomenon with hits like "Hey Joe" and "Purple Haze." His rendition of the "Star-Spangled Banner" at Woodstock in 1969 is etched in rock history. Hendrix expanded the range and vocabulary of rock and blues guitar with his technique as well as his use of guitar effects such as feedback, distortion, and the wah-wah pedal.

Album pick: *Jimi Hendrix: Blues*, Sony Legacy, 2014. Jimi Hendrix, the blues—enough said.

John Lee Hooker   August 22, 1917–June 21, 2001

The son of a sharecropper, Hooker rose to prominence performing an electric guitar-style adaptation of Delta blues. He often incorporated other elements, including talking blues, into his music, and developed his own driving-rhythm boogie style. Hooker rarely played with a standard beat but instead changed tempo to fit the needs of the song.

He collaborated with several rock musicians, which widened his exposure to new audiences. Hooker recorded an album with the American blues band Canned Heat in 1970, and also collaborated on albums with Steve Miller, Elvin Bishop, Van Morrison, Carlos Santana, and Bonnie Raitt.

Album Pick: *I'm John Lee Hooker*, originally released in 1959, reissue, Charly Records, 2003. Recorded in the late 1950s, these tracks are Hooker in his prime, a collection of many of his best-loved songs without any frills—just solid blues.

Lightnin' Hopkins   March 15, 1912–January 30, 1982

Lightnin' Hopkins' blues education began when he was eight years old and met Blind Lemon Jefferson at a Texas church picnic. The blues great took a liking to the boy, and Hopkins began accompanying him on guitar at informal church gatherings, reportedly the only one Jefferson would let do this.

Hopkins was "discovered" during the folk revival of the early 1960s when blues singer/guitarists were being introduced to a larger audience. He made his debut at Carnegie Hall on October 14, 1960 alongside Joan Baez and Pete Seeger. Through the 1960s and into the '70s, he released several albums and toured, playing at folk festivals, clubs, and college campuses. Hopkins developed a blues style that focused on complex fingerpicking and guitar effects to back up his singing.

Album pick: *Lightnin' Hopkins*, Smithsonian Folkways, 1992. Originally released under the name *The Roots of Lightnin' Hopkins* in 1959, the album was recorded in a one-room apartment using only one microphone—a bare-bones masterpiece.

Son House   March 21, 1902–October 19, 1988

Son House played guitar in the Delta blues style emphasizing passionate vocals and slide guitar work. He shunned the blues at first, given his calling as a preacher and pastor. But according to legend, he changed his mind at age twenty-five after hearing someone play blues bottleneck slide guitar, and soon developed his own style. He was a formative influence on Robert Johnson and Muddy Waters.

House gave up the music business but in 1964 was encouraged to relearn his repertoire, and he began performing in coffeehouses and at folk festivals. He went on to record several albums.

Album pick: *Father of the Delta Blues: The Complete 1965 Sessions*, Sony, 1992. After being "rediscovered" by the folk-blues revival movement in the 1960s, Son House was given studio time to rerecord some of his best work. The results are wonderful.

Howlin' Wolf   June 10, 1910–January 10, 1976

Howlin' Wolf, originally from Mississippi, was one of the best-known Chicago-style blues musicians. Several of his songs, including "Smokestack Lightnin'," "Killing Floor," and "Spoonful," have become blues standards. During the blues revival in the 1950s and '60s, Howlin' Wolf gained renewed appreciation.

He was an imposing performer, standing 6-foot-3 inches tall and weighing close to 300 pounds. His name, he explained, came from his grandfather who would tell him stories about wolves near where they lived and warn him that if he misbehaved, the "howling wolves" would get him.

In 1930, he met blues great Charley Patton, whom he would listen to standing outside clubs where Patton was playing. Eventually, they became friends and played around the Delta together. Patton gave him guitar tips and performance tricks that became part of Howlin' Wolf's act.

Album pick: *Moanin' in the Moonlight*, originally released in 1959, reissue, Soul Jam Records, 2012. Packed with the best cuts from Howlin' Wolf's recordings of Chicago blues, which he helped to define. A must for any blues collection.

Mississippi John Hurt   July 3, 1893–November 2, 1966

I remember the first time I heard Mississippi John Hurt. I was thumbing through the record racks of the hippest guitar and record shop in Santa Fe, named The Candyman (after a Hurt song), when the most amazing blues guitar fingerpicking I had ever heard wafted from the store's speakers. I've been a die-hard fan ever since. Hurt taught himself to play guitar at age nine. But until he was "discovered" in the 1960s, he was a sharecropper and farmer. As a singer/guitarist, he played a combination of Delta blues, country blues, and folk music. Hurt played in basic keys, sometimes using open tunings and a slide. I am only one of his legions of fans. His playing influenced generations of guitarists, and his songs have been covered by many contemporary artists including Bob Dylan, Jerry Garcia, Taj Mahal, and Gillian Welch.

Album pick: *Mississippi John Hurt: Today!* Vanguard Records, original 1966 recording, remastered, 1990. The gentle genius of fingerstyle guitar picking at his finest.

Elmore James   January 27, 1918–May 24, 1963

James was known as "the King of the Slide Guitar." His unique guitar style was noted for its loud amplification and his stirring voice. James's powerful guitar sound came from a modified, hollow body traditional acoustic guitar. His guitar accompaniment was as raw and expressive as his voice, usually using a bottleneck blues technique. He was influenced by Muddy Waters, Howlin' Wolf, and B.B. King, and in turn, he influenced many future blues guitarists. His songs have been covered by the Rolling Stones, the Allman Brothers Band, George Thorogood, and Stevie Ray Vaughan, among others. Early in his career, Jimi Hendrix went by the name "Maurice James" and later "Jimmy James" as a tribute to Elmore James.

Album pick: *The Sky Is Crying: The History of Elmore James*, Rhino, 1993. If you are a fan of blues slide guitar, this collection is a must.

Skip James   June 9, 1902–October 3, 1969

Skip James was an American Delta blues singer and guitarist known for his minor-sounding blues and advanced fingerpicking style.

James first recorded for Paramount Records in 1931, but the recordings were nearly lost until his music became popular again during the 1960s blues and folk revival. After this, James appeared at folk and blues festivals, gave concerts around the country, and recorded several albums for various labels.

Album pick: *Skip James Today!* Vanguard, 1991. Sometimes not given the attention of other blues greats, James shows he belongs in that league with this stunning album of Delta blues recorded in the mid-1960s.

Blind Lemon Jefferson   1893–December 19, 1929

Blind Lemon Jefferson made over a hundred recordings which highlighted his high-pitched singing and complex, fast-paced blues guitar playing. His recording of "Black Snake Moan" in 1926 was one of the first rural blues hits. He mentored another blues great, T-Bone Walker, in exchange for Walker's services as his seeing guide. Jefferson's success as a singer/guitarist in the 1920s opened the door for other blues players. But the life of a vagabond musician was not easy, and he froze to death during a Chicago snowstorm on December 19, 1929. Jefferson has been called the "Father of the Texas Blues," and influenced later blues players including Lead Belly and Lightnin' Hopkins.

Album pick: *King of the Country Blues*, Yazoo, 1985. Many of the songs on this album are taken from old 78 recordings, but it's still easy to appreciate Jefferson's inventive guitar work and the haunting vocal quality that made him one of the most successful blues artists of his time.

Robert Johnson   May 8, 1911–August 16, 1938

Any review of legendary blues guitarists must include Robert Johnson. When I listen to any of the twenty-nine recordings he made during his short career, it feels like a bolt of lightning sizzling through the speakers. Johnson's heart-rending falsetto and masterful guitar accompaniment sound as vital today as in 1937. Though he was only twenty-seven when he died, he has influenced many blues and rock guitarists including Eric Clapton, who called him "the most important blues singer that ever lived."

Johnson's guitar style was in the Delta blues tradition, but what made his playing unique was his ability to integrate so many other influences, including slide, country, jazz, ragtime, and swing. His technique was so complex that it often sounded as if two guitarists were playing. According to legend, Johnson promised his soul to the devil in exchange for mastery of the guitar, a tale dramatized in the 1986 movie *Crossroads*.

Album pick: *Robert Johnson: The Complete Recordings*, Columbia/Legacy, 1990. The album contains every known recording Johnson made.

Albert King   April 25, 1923–December 21, 1992

Albert King is one of the three performers (together with B.B. King and Freddie King) who are known as the "Kings of the Blues." He claimed to be a half-brother to B.B. King, but B.B. denied it. Nevertheless, Albert King named his guitar "Lucy" in tribute to B.B. King's guitar, "Lucille."

A passionate blues guitarist, Albert King emphasized bending notes in his solos on the Gibson Flying V guitar that he used in concerts. His deep, emotional voice perfectly mirrored his intense guitar playing. Though he was left-handed, King usually played right-handed guitars flipped upside-down. His most popular albums, *Born Under a Bad Sign* and *Live Wire/ Blues Power,* inspired many blues guitarists in the late 1960s, including Jimi Hendrix, Stevie Ray Vaughan, and Eric Clapton.

Album pick: *Born Under a Bad Sign,* original recording 1967, reissued, remastered Stax, 2013. Albert King sizzles on this album of electric blues with an all-star backing band including Steve Cropper, Booker T, Donald "Duck" Dunn, and Isaac Hayes.

B.B. King   September 16, 1925–May 14, 2015

B.B. King is perhaps the most loved blues guitarist/singer in history. It takes only a few notes to recognize his melodic blues phrasing and signature string-bending which has been copied by generations of guitarists. King seamlessly mixed jazz, swing, and pop into his unique sound. He played two hundred fifty to three hundred shows a year for most of his career, carrying his music to people all over the world. If there was anyone who deserved the titles of "Ambassador of the Blues" and "King of the Blues," it was B.B. King. His awards and honors are too numerous to list. His influence includes many great guitarists including Jimi Hendrix, Eric Clapton, Jimmy Page, Robert Cray, Duane Allman, and Stevie Ray Vaughan.

Album pick: *Live at the Regal,* Geffen Records, 1997. Recorded live at the Regal Theatre in 1964, this is one of the most powerful live blues performances ever recorded.

Freddie King   September 3, 1934–December 28, 1976

Freddie King was an influential guitarist with hits for Federal Records in the early 1960s, using a guitar style based on Texas blues and Chicago blues influences. Sneaking into South Side nightclubs, he could hear blues performed by Muddy Waters, Howlin' Wolf, T-Bone Walker, Elmore James, and Sonny Boy Williamson.

King used both a plastic thumb pick and a metal index-finger pick.

Later in his career, he performed alongside the big rock acts of the day like Eric Clapton and Grand Funk Railroad (whose song "We're an American Band" mentions King in its lyrics).

Album pick: *Burglar,* 1992, Polydor. King and a bevy of guest artists showcase his electric blues guitar prowess and vocals. Recorded two years before his death, it finally gave him the studio attention and production he deserved.

Lead Belly   January 20, 1888–December 6, 1949

Lead Belly played both blues and folk music on his oversized Stella twelve-string guitar. Some recordings and publications spelled his name as "Leadbelly," but he wrote it as Lead Belly. Born Huddie William Ledbetter, Lead Belly used a thumb pick along with his other fingerpicking to provide a walking bass line, and occasionally to strum. Sometimes he tuned his strings down lower than standard tuning to give his guitar a deeper, fuller sound.

Lead Belly was promoted as the convict who sang his way out of prison, once being pardoned and released after writing a song to the governor seeking his freedom. He was imprisoned many times for violent crimes from 1915–1939. But after his final release in 1940, he became popular appearing on a CBS radio show broadcast nationwide. Lead Belly often performed in New York City nightclubs with musicians such as Josh White, Sonny Terry, Brownie McGhee, Woody Guthrie, and Pete Seeger.

Album pick: *Midnight Special: The Library of Congress Recordings, Vol. 1*, Rounder Records, 1992. Lead Belly's blues guitar playing is jaw-dropping despite the fact that the recording was made in 1934 by Alan Lomax while Lead Belly was an inmate at Angola Penitentiary in Louisiana.

John Mayall   November 29, 1933

John Mayall has been testifying for the blues for over sixty years. His eminent Bluesbreakers band lineups have included some of the most outstanding blues guitarists of his time, including Eric Clapton, Peter Green, Mick Taylor, and Harvey Mandel. Although Mayall is widely acknowledged as a superb blues multi-instrumentalist, singer, and songwriter, perhaps his most enduring legacy is the careers he has helped launch.

Album pick: *Back to the Roots*, Polydor, 1971. In this relatively overlooked double album, Mayall invited members of his former bands to contribute cameo appearances. Those who answered the call include Eric Clapton, Mick Taylor, Harvey Mandel, Johnny Almond, and Sugarcane Harris. Mayall encourages his guests to improvise blues licks liberally throughout the album, making it a showcase of blues technique.

John Mayer   October 16, 1977

Although John Mayer has achieved a high level of commercial success as a pop/rock musician, he is rooted in the blues. He continues to carry the blues torch through his guitar playing influenced by masters such as B.B. King and Buddy Guy. He has played beside these and other blues giants including Eric Clapton. Mayer solidified his reputation as a blues player with his band, the John Mayer Trio, in 2005. He continues to be a respected influence on up-and-coming blues guitarists.

Album pick: *Try*, original release, Columbia, 2005. In this live concert album recorded with his trio November 10, 2005, Mayer returns to his blues roots, showcasing his impressive chops.

Memphis Minnie   June 3, 1897–August 6, 1973

Memphis Minnie was a force in the blues scene from the 1920s to the '50s. With her early adoption of the electric guitar and her mighty singing voice, she led the transition from rural to urban blues.

By the age of thirteen, Minnie had already left home to play on street corners in Memphis, and from 1916 to 1920, she was playing the blues with the Ringling Brothers Circus across the South. She began her recording career in the 1930s, and by the early '40s, she was playing the blues on an electric guitar. In 1941, Minnie recorded her biggest hit, "Me and My Chauffeur Blues." She continued to record and tour through most of the 1950s until her health began to decline.

Album pick: *Queen of the Blues*, Columbia, 1997. These recordings, made from 1929 to '46, span Memphis Minnie's remarkable career. Her accomplished and innovative blues guitar picking and powerful singing place her side-by-side with the male blues artist who were her contemporaries. Minnie was the real deal.

Jimmy Page   January 9, 1944

Jimmy Page is best known as the lead guitarist for the English supergroup Led Zeppelin. He is admired as a great riff creator and for his rock guitar style which borrowed from blues, country, folk, and other influences. His signature double-neck guitar was part of his persona. Page began as a studio musician in London in the mid-1960s. He played with the Yardbirds from 1966 to 1968, when he began Led Zeppelin. Page's early influences include blues greats Buddy Guy, B.B. King, and Elmore James, and he also admired Scotty Moore and James Burton, who both backed up Elvis Presley at different times in Elvis's career.

Album pick: *Led Zeppelin II*, Atlantic. Released in 1969, the album is based on reworked classic blues songs featuring Page's extended blues-based guitar riffs and solos. It would become the template for heavy metal, blues/rock albums for decades to come.

Charley Patton 1887–1934

Charley Patton was one of the early innovators of blues guitar and has been referred to as "The Father of the Delta Blues." Many musicians traveled to Sunflower County, Mississippi, to learn the blues from Patton. He developed his slide guitar technique using open tuning and employed the blunt edge of a knife or the neck of a glass bottle to create his sound. Patton was a versatile guitar player, and his repertoire included blues, country and "hillbilly" music, and popular ballads of the day. He was also a showman, playing his guitar between his legs and over his head. Patton's fancy strumming and slide technique complemented his gravelly voiced singing, and earned him a reputation as one of the best bluesmen around.

Album pick: *Founder of the Delta Blues*, Yazoo, 1969. Twenty-six of Patton's classic Delta blues songs recorded between 1929 and 1934 are on this album. They highlight the best of his skilled slide guitar work.

Bonnie Raitt November 8, 1949

Bonnie Raitt is proof that great blues guitar playing has no ethnic or gender boundaries. Perhaps best known for her blues bottleneck slide guitar style, she has toured much of her career with a customized Fender Stratocaster that has defined her sound. Raitt's blues guitar playing first received notice when she performed at the Philly Folk Festival in 1970 with blues legend Mississippi Fred McDowell. Throughout her career, blues has remained an essential part of her musical repertoire.

Album pick: *Nick of Time*, Capitol, 1989. After almost two decades toiling as an underappreciated blues guitarist/singer, Raitt reached No. 1 on the charts with this album and won four Grammys.

Jimmy Reed September 6, 1925–August 29, 1976

Reed was an American blues musician and songwriter whose style of electric blues was popular with a wide audience. He influenced such musicians as Elvis Presley, Hank Williams Jr., and the Rolling Stones, who recorded several of his songs. Others who recorded Reed's songs include Elvis Presley, the Animals, Van Morrison's group Them, and the Yardbirds.

Album pick: *Jimmy Reed at Carnegie Hall*, VeeJay Records, 1974. This is not a live album, nor was it recorded at Carnegie Hall. What it is in reality is a collection of Reed's best material. A nice collection (false advertising aside) of catchy blues songs.

Keith Richards   December 18, 1943

Keith Richards, guitarist for the Rolling Stones, has always remained loyal to his blues roots. His body of distinctive riffs is etched in the memories of rock and blues lovers everywhere. His focus has always been on chording, rhythm guitar, and interplay with other guitarists rather than on showy individual virtuosity. Richards' style weaves together lead and rhythm guitar playing, and he also is known for his use of open tunings and his acoustic guitar work.

Album pick: *The Rolling Stones: Blue and Lonesome,* Interscope, 2016. It took only three days to record but five decades of preparation. The Stones go back to their roots and play the blues.

Taj Mahal   May 17, 1942

Taj Mahal has been redefining the blues for over half a century by reshaping its sound in combination with world music influences.

He collaborated with fellow blues guitarist Ry Cooder in 1964 to form Rising Sons, and also worked with prominent blues guitarists like Howlin' Wolf and Muddy Waters. As a soloist, his blues guitar technique is featured in albums such as *Taj Mahal* in 1968, *The Natch'l Blues* in 1969, and *Giant Step/De Old Folks at Home,* in 1969. In 1972, he wrote the score for the movie *Sounder.* More recently, he has recorded a full array of albums synthesizing blues and world music.

Taj Mahal is also a scholar of the blues and world music in general, which has led him to do research and other types of music history projects.

Album pick: *Taj Mahal,* Columbia, 1968. This album, recorded in 1967, contains a blues style reminiscent of the 1930s and '40s. It is a loving tribute to the legacy of the blues featuring Taj Mahal's slide guitar playing and contributions from guests such as Ry Cooder and Jesse Ed Davis.

Derek Trucks   June 8, 1979

Derek Trucks is a blues guitar child prodigy who had performed alongside Buddy Guy by his thirteenth birthday. He was groomed in the guitar style of Southern blues rock. He became a member of the Allman Brothers Band in 1999, following in the footsteps of his father, Butch Trucks, who was the band's original drummer.

Trucks formed the Derek Trucks Band in 1994 and has continued playing music rooted in the blues but also reaching out toward rock, jazz, world music, and other musical forms. He cites many blues and jazz musicians as influences including Duane Allman, Elmore James, Charlie Christian, and Miles Davis.

Album pick: *Already Free,* Legacy 2009. Trucks recorded this album in his home studio, and the result is a relaxed atmosphere that enhances his blues slide guitar and formidable acoustic guitar skills. Aided by a strong horn section and the contributions of his stellar band, Trucks creates a blues-influenced album that is a joy to listen to.

Stevie Ray Vaughan   October 3, 1954–August 27, 1990

It's almost impossible to tune in to a rock radio station in America without hearing Stevie Ray Vaughan's blues guitar mastery in short order. He fueled the blues revival of the 1980s with sold-out concerts and gold records that were a tribute to his accomplished guitar playing. Vaughan's influences included Albert King, Freddie King, Muddy Waters, and Jimi Hendrix. However, his main influence was Lonnie Mack, from whom he learned many of his signature techniques. He toured and recorded with his band Double Trouble from 1983–1990 before he was killed in a helicopter accident after a show.

Album pick: *Texas Flood,* Sony Legacy Edition, 2013. Originally released in 1983 as Vaughan's debut album, it was recorded in only three days. The album made the blues cool again in the 1980s and sparked another surge of this timeless music.

T-Bone Walker   May 28, 1910–March 16, 1975

T-Bone Walker was an early pioneer of the electric blues guitar sound, blending Delta and Texas Blues. He started his career at fifteen, quickly becoming a regular performer on the blues circuit. Blind Lemon Jefferson was a family friend when Walker was growing up in Texas, and he eventually became Jefferson's protégé and would guide him around town for his gigs.

Walker is known for writing one of the most revered songs in blues history in 1947, "Stormy Monday." B.B. King cited the song as one of his inspirations for getting an electric guitar. "Stormy Monday" was also a favorite live number of the Allman Brothers Band. Another Walker admirer was Jimi Hendrix, who imitated Walker's trick of playing the guitar with his teeth.

Album pick: *T-Bone Blues,* originally released 1959, reissue, Atlantic, 2014. These recordings were made in the 1950s, but the sound quality is remarkably good. T-Bone's blues guitar style is understated but powerful.

Muddy Waters April 4, 1913–April 30, 1983

Muddy Waters made the blues electric! He was a pioneer of electric blues guitar and a major inspiration for many rock and blues guitarists. He also was the inspiration for what came to be known as the Chicago blues style in the 1950s. His songs "Hoochie Coochie Man" and "Mannish Boy" are classics to blues lovers. His sound was basically the Delta blues electrified. Muddy Waters' protégés include Eric Clapton, Keith Richards, Jimi Hendrix, Duane Allman, and Jimmy Page. Richards has said that the Rolling Stones named themselves after his song "Rollin' Stone."

Album pick: *Hard Again*, Sony Music Canada Inc. 2011. In 1977, Muddy Waters hooked up with Johnny Winter as his producer for this recording which reestablished him as one of the all-time masters of the blues.

Johnny Winter February 23, 1944–July 16, 2014

Listening to Johnny Winter's And/Live album recorded at the Filmore East in 1970 is a lesson in blues fire that still holds its own. A generation of blues guitarists has spent many an hour deciphering the interplay between Winter and co-guitarist Rick Derringer on this album. Winter is best known for his high energy blues-oriented concerts and albums in the late 1960s and early '70s. His repertoire included songs by blues masters like B.B. King, Sonny Boy Williamson, and Chuck Berry. Johnny and his brother Edgar, also an accomplished musician, were both born with albinism, which only added to their riveting stage presence.

Album pick: *Johnny Winter And/Live*, Legacy, 2008. Winter and Derringer trading burning blues licks—too hot to touch!

Guitar Guide for Beginners

Some readers of this book will be picking up a guitar for the first time. If you are among them, this section is filled with the information you need to get started.

You will find there are many ways to use this section, such as solo guitar, joining with other musicians, or playing along with recorded music. Experiment to see how they fit with the music you want to be playing.

And when what you learn gives you that irresistible urge to plunge with it into the glory of the blues—well, that's what this book is here for.

Your Most Important Instrument: Your Hands

No instrument in your guitar-playing odyssey is as important as your hands. Their training and care are not something to take for granted. Here are a few points to consider about these amazing appendages.

I often hear beginning guitarists complain that their hands are too large or small to navigate the guitar easily enough or that their fingers are too stiff or uncoordinated. In the vast majority of cases, aspiring guitarists have perfectly adequate fingers and hands to play just about anything, and this is not as much of an issue as they initially think it is.

I like to tell students that if Muddy Waters' big hands didn't keep him from playing the guitar, they shouldn't be worried about theirs. On the other side of the spectrum are many child prodigies with small hands and fingers who perform at an amazing level. Django Reinhart, the great jazz/gypsy guitarist, managed to play without the use of two fingers. In some ways, we all must work around our limitations, but this should not stop us from reaching our full potential as guitarists.

Fingernails

Your nails require constant vigilance. Basically, you need to keep them short enough on your left hand (assuming you're a right-handed guitarist) so they don't touch the fingerboard when you are pressing down on the frets. The fingernails on your fingerpicking or strumming hand are a different story. You will generally want these to be on the long side to get the best tone. Whether you're sweeping across the strings with the nails of your strumming hand or picking individual strings by hitting them with the fleshy part of your finger followed by the nail, a slightly long fingernail will give you the nicest sound.

It's easy to forget to keep your nails clipped, and you often don't notice it until you pick up your guitar and start playing. Having a pair of nail clippers in your guitar case is a good way to make sure you don't have to struggle through an uncomfortable session with fingernails that keep getting in the way as you play. It also saves you from the unpleasant alternative of chewing on your nails before a gig.

Sore Fingers

The guitar is a physically demanding instrument, and sore fingers are simply part of the bargain. It is important not to add to your misery by having a guitar that is difficult to play, which usually occurs because of "high action," which means the strings are too high above the fingerboard. This is the biggest obstacle that I see beginning guitarists face. An instrument that is too difficult to play will quickly discourage even the most enthusiastic guitarist.

There are no real shortcuts to build up finger strength or avoid finger soreness when you first start playing. But as you practice, your fingers will keep getting stronger. Overall strength does not translate into finger strength; body builders have no advantage over anyone else. Generally, almost everyone's fingers are just fine; they just need training. Your fingers will become able to do things that once seemed impossible. The idea of building up guitar "calluses" is a bit of an exaggeration. Your fingers will need to toughen up, but nothing as major as that. After two or three weeks of practice, you will find that your fingers have already begun feeling better.

Left-Handed Guitarists

If you are left-handed, the choice of whether to play the guitar left-handed or right-handed will be a personal decision. You will have to decide what feels more natural. Can you cope with chord diagrams and scales that are written backward? Some guitarists like Jimi Hendrix and Paul McCartney preferred to play left-handed despite the obstacles. Other left-handers like Paul Simon and Mark Knopfler switched to playing right-handed with spectacular results. No one else knows the best thing for you to do; only you can decide.

Identifying Your Fingers

Working on the assumption that you are playing the guitar right-handed, we will refer to your right hand as your strumming hand and your left hand as the chording hand. Chords are the combination of notes that are produced when you hold down more than one string at a time with your chording hand and strum them simultaneously.

To identify your fingers individually, a system for naming each one helps. The same designations will be used for the fingers of your strumming and chording hands: The thumb will be called the "T" finger, the index finger the "1" finger, the middle finger the "2," the ring finger the "3," and the little finger the "4" finger. (See illustration on next page.)

Gaining Hand Strength and Facility

Students often ask if anything can be done to strengthen their hands or make their fingers more flexible. My advice has always been to simply practice the guitar more. There is no better way to develop the ligaments, joints, muscles, and tendons in your hands and fingers than to simply

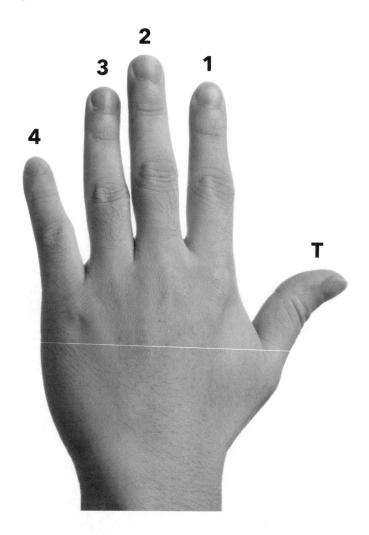

play the guitar. Hand exercises or squeezing rubber balls are poor substitutes. Often, the best guitarists are not those who buy expensive guitars or take more lessons. The ones who advance fastest are those who have a guitar in their hands most often.

Getting to Know Your Axe: Your Guitar
Acoustic guitars

Generally, these are played without being plugged into an amplifier (although sometimes pickups are installed to allow amplification). The two basic types are the "folk" guitar, which has steel strings, and the "classical" guitar, with nylon strings.

Although both are considered acoustic guitars, they are quite different. The steel-string guitar is generally larger, heavier, and made of thicker wood than a nylon-string guitar. A steel-string guitar has six metal strings whereas the strings of the classical guitar have a nylon core. Even though the lower strings on a nylon-string guitar may look like they are made of metal, in reality, a metal exterior is wound around their nylon-based core. Classical guitars also generally have a wider, shorter neck.

A broad generalization can help to explain the differences in construction: Folk guitars are meant to be strummed with a pick, and classical guitars are generally picked with the fingers. With a folk guitar, more volume is typically generated through an aggressive strumming technique using a pick, and a heavier, sturdier instrument is required. In contrast,

Steel-string guitar, left, and nylon string guitar

a classical guitar must be made of thinner wood, so the guitar won't dampen the sound and will optimize the volume of a quieter fingerpicking technique.

Although this is usually the case, there certainly are exceptions: fingerpicking folk guitarists like James Taylor and musicians who strum classical guitars, such as Willie Nelson. That's the beauty of music; creative artists are always crossing genres and using instruments differently to create unique sounds.

One thing to keep in mind is that you can't make a folk guitar into a classical guitar or vice versa simply by swapping the strings. A folk guitar with nylon strings will sound very dull and deadened because the body is too thick to resonate adequately. A classical guitar with steel strings will likewise produce a poor-quality sound and can actually be damaged because the tension of steel strings on a guitar neck is much greater than that of nylon strings. Most folk guitars have a metal truss rod that runs through the neck to withstand this tension, but classical guitars do not. If you want the sound (and music) of the other type of guitar, you'll have to get one; you can't make it from the one you have.

Basic Acoustic Guitar Features

Each part of an acoustic guitar plays an important role in producing its sound. The large, hourglass-shaped body resonates, with the sound escaping from the hole in the middle of the body. The type of wood, its thickness, and the finish that is applied have a great effect on the sound of each guitar.

This sound is produced when the vibration of a string is transmitted to the body through the "bridge," which sits on the body below the sound hole. Thin, wooden strands lie underneath the front of the guitar for support and spread the transfer of vibrations to produce sound across the front of the guitar body.

Usually, the front of the body is made from thinly cut spruce, with a hardwood like maple used for the back and sides. Vibrations from the front of the guitar are amplified as they bounce off the denser back and escape out the sound hole.

The neck of the guitar is the section extending from the body where chords and notes are fingered. Crossing the neck are the frets. When you press a string between these metal bars, picking or strumming will produce notes.

Above the neck is the headstock with the tuning pegs that tighten or loosen the strings to raise or lower their pitch. Below the tuning pegs is a thick, white bone or plastic piece that crosses the neck above the first fret. This is called the "nut," and serves to hold the guitar's six strings off the neck so they can vibrate and produce sound.

At the other end of the strings, the bridge serves a similar purpose by keeping them off the neck. This is a piece of wood attached to the body below the sound hole which has a thin white piece of bone or plastic extending upward.

Parts of the Guitar

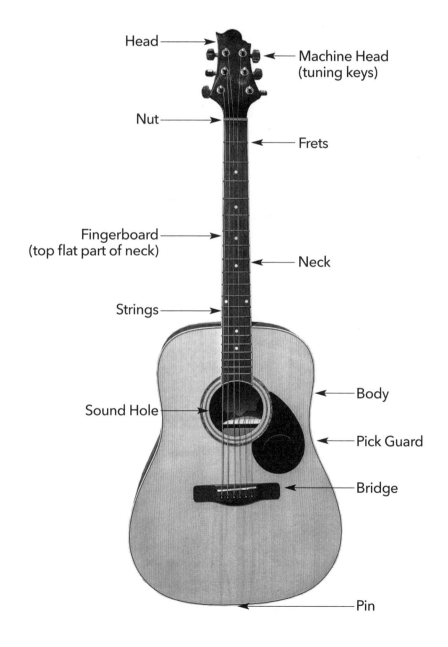

Head

Machine Head (tuning keys)

Nut

Frets

Fingerboard (top flat part of neck)

Neck

Strings

Body

Sound Hole

Pick Guard

Bridge

Pin

Now that you know the basic parts of the guitar, here are some important areas to pay attention to in choosing a guitar you will be happy with.

Choosing a Guitar

A guitar that will make a great companion doesn't have to be expensive. Many good instruments for the beginning to intermediate guitarist can be bought without breaking the bank. Several fine guitars are available in the $150–$300 range.

One possibility to have in mind is buying a used guitar, which can be a great way to get the most value for your buck. Guitars don't generally decline in quality over time if they are not abused. In fact, a used guitar will often have better sound than a new one because the wood has had an opportunity to age and settle. If you buy a new guitar from a music dealer and turn around the next day and try to sell it back, you'll be lucky to get half of what you paid. Garage sales, flea markets, and classified ads are great places to start. You might even be one of the lucky folks who pick up a vintage instrument that becomes a family heirloom for a rock bottom price.

Don't be fooled by appearances; sometimes that old, dusty guitar with the cigarette burns is a priceless gem. Of course, if you have the money, there are beautiful instruments made by fine craftsmen throughout the country that are just waiting for an owner. My suggestion is to never buy a guitar without the assistance of an experienced guitarist who can advise you. It would be like buying a used car without a mechanic's inspection.

Perhaps of all the qualities in a guitar to consider, action is the most important. This refers to how high above the neck your strings sit, which determines how much pressure you have to apply with your fingers to get a clear sound. You can live with a guitar that doesn't have the most stellar tone, but it is almost impossible to make any headway with a guitar that is painful to play. Eventually, it will lead to very sore fingers and little desire to pick up your guitar at all.

I recommend choosing a guitar with strings that are close to the neck and take relatively little effort to press down. Later, as your fingers get stronger, you may wish to raise the action for better sound. This is an area where there is always a compromise. I find that light or extra light strings are best for novice guitarists playing steel-string guitars. Medium-gauge strings are much too hard to play on for the average beginner.

Keep in mind that almost all guitars that come off the rack in music stores need to have their action adjusted because it is too high. This is just as true for guitars costing thousands of dollars as for less-expensive models. Having a guitar technician adjust your guitar's action and lower the strings as much as possible without getting too many buzzes (always a compromise) is something you should definitely invest in. The technician also will adjust your nut, frets, bridge, and neck where necessary.

A good guitar repair technician can do wonders with your guitar's action. Often lowering the nut and/or the bridge can result in better action. It is also important to check that the neck is straight. Steel-string guitars often have a truss rod which can be adjusted to straighten the neck. If making these fixes is too difficult or expensive, sometimes a quick, cheap solution to lower your action is to put a capo (a mechanical bar that holds down all the strings) on the first fret of your guitar and act as if the second fret is actually the first.

Folk Guitar or Classical?

The decision to buy a folk (steel string) or classical (nylon string) guitar will depend on several factors. The first is the type of music you are most interested in playing. A folk guitar is more often used for strumming with a pick than a classical guitar. Thus, rock, uptempo country, and folk or blues music may be more suited to a folk guitar. Bending notes is also much more effective on a steel-string guitar.

A classical guitar is especially well suited for fingerpicking and classical or flamenco solo pieces. Ballads, gentler folk music, soft rock, and instrumentals are especially well-suited for the classical guitar.

Though these generalities about the two types of acoustic guitar are true, keep in mind that you can play any kind of music on either one; it just depends on the sound you are after and your imagination.

In regard to playability, the classical guitar has a wider, shorter neck, and it can be more difficult to reach the higher notes at the top of the neck. Nylon strings are usually easier on the fingertips at first and may not be as painful for beginning guitarists. The folk guitar usually has a larger body and a longer, thinner neck. Steel strings tend to be a little harder on the fingers until the skin toughens up with practice.

The Electric Guitar

The backbone of contemporary blues and rock music is the electric guitar. It is hard to imagine modern blues without the soaring lead guitar lines of the electric guitar. If this is your inspiration, you may want to acquire an electric guitar.

The technological breakthrough that led to the development of the electric guitar was the "pickup." Early innovators got the idea of wrapping a coil of wire around a magnet; when it was put underneath the guitar strings, their vibrations made an electrical signal that could be amplified. This created a sound with more volume that could be sustained longer. Additionally, the electric guitar sound could be manipulated to produce new and creative variations of tones, like distortion and feedback. Guitarists were quick to use these new possibilities—innovations that transformed the guitar into a national cultural icon.

This experimentation with electric guitars began in the 1920s and '30s. The Rickenbacker Company out of Los Angeles marketed the earliest electric guitar in 1931, aiming to reproduce the sound of a Hawaiian steel guitar. It was the first guitar with an electro-magnetic pickup and became an inspiration for future electric guitar development. In 1936, Gibson created the ES-150 guitar which used a pickup for amplification, but it was not widely accepted. Another, more-refined early prototype was created in 1941 by Les Paul, a famous guitarist of his time. It was still a crude version of the modern electric guitar, though, so much so that he named his creation "The Log."

In the early 1950s, music began to undergo dramatic changes with the advent of rock 'n' roll and rhythm and blues. As styles changed, the electric guitar began to play a larger role in the landscape of American music. It achieved national prominence after the introduction of two models that caught the fancy of young musicians across the country. In 1952, the Gibson company developed an electric guitar designed by and named after the early electric guitar innovator, Les Paul. In 1954, Leo Fender began marketing a solid body electric guitar called the "Stratocaster." Both instruments would become the gold standard for years to come as rock 'n' roll grew into a national phenomenon. As it did, the guitar grew from being a backup instrument to becoming the instrument of choice for countless young people forming garage bands all across America.

Learning to play on an electric guitar is identical to learning on an acoustic guitar. But keep in mind that not only your progress but also your mistakes will be amplified! You will also need to buy an amplifier in addition to your guitar. Electric guitar models and amplifiers come in a mind-boggling array of choices. Your decision as to what is right for you will depend on the type of music you want to play and whether you want to play on your own or join a band with a drummer and other instruments. If your goal is to join a band, you may need a more-powerful amplifier.

Strings

If you don't know or can't remember the last time the strings on your guitar were changed, it is definitely time to replace them. If you're not happy with the sound of your guitar, buying a new one may not be needed; a simple change of strings can give you a great new tone.

When you buy new strings, go with inexpensive ones; most beginning guitarists can't tell the difference. Wait until you're booked at Carnegie Hall before you buy the most-expensive set. And don't be afraid to change your own strings; it's not that difficult. Have an experienced guitarist string one for you and copy his or her technique, or you can refer to a tutorial on YouTube. Don't take all the strings off when you change strings; leave at least one on to use as an example for stringing the others. Strings should be changed at least every six months, sooner if you play often.

A Final Note

Whatever guitar you finally decide on, don't cut corners in buying a case for it. You will want a sturdy, well-made hard-shell case to protect your investment.

Nothing Sounds Good Until You Can Do This: Tuning the Guitar

Tuning is one of the most important aspects to focus on for the beginning guitarist. A guitar that is poorly tuned will produce an unpleasant sound even if the guitarist does everything else right. It takes time to train one's ear to tune guitar strings well, especially if you have never played another musical instrument. My recommendation is that every guitarist acquire an electronic tuner, which has become very inexpensive. It requires no ear training, and all you have to do is turn the tuning peg for each string until the device tells you it is in tune by lining up a visual indicator of some kind, or perhaps a light will come on.

Even experienced guitarists rely on electronic tuners, since it is more time-consuming to tune by ear. If professionals do this for recording and concerts, don't feel like you are cheating. The more you use the tuner, the more it will help to train your ear, making you more accustomed to what a well-tuned guitar sounds like. Older methods for tuning a guitar, such as the pitch pipe and tuning fork, are hard for many guitarists to use. Their sounds are so different from a guitar's that it is difficult to match up the pitch.

Don't fall for the old saying "close enough for folk music." Guitars should always be as well-tuned as possible. It can be very confusing at first when you try to tune. Is the pitch that you are hearing lower or higher than what is intended? Which way do you turn the tuning peg to lower or raise the pitch? At first, finding the right pitch can be like trying to find an exact spot on an invisible line that stretches from the floor to the ceiling.

Tuning a guitar using only its strings is the traditional method. This is a good option when you are playing and don't have time to stop and tune in any other way. For this to work, you need at least one string that is in tune with the rest of the world so your tuning matches that of other instruments (obviously less of a problem if you are playing alone).

Here's how to tune a guitar using only its other strings. The more you practice doing this, the better your ear will get. For most people, being able to hear the correct pitch is an acquired skill, not something they're born with. Although it may be frustrating at first, keep trying and you will slowly find that your ear is improving.

Tuning

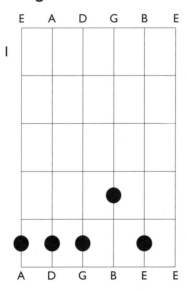

Traditional String Tuning Method

Step One: Press down on the fifth fret of the sixth string, pick that string, and listen to the note that is produced. Then play the fifth string open and listen to that note to determine if the pitch is the same. If it isn't, you will need to adjust the open fifth string by tightening or loosening the tension with the tuning peg at the top of your guitar. Turn the peg slowly, raising or lowering the pitch, until it matches the pitch of the sixth string when you've pressed it down on the fifth fret. Humming the notes as you tune may help you hear when your strings are tuned correctly. When you get the pitches to match, the fifth and sixth string are in tune with each other.

Step Two: Repeat Step One, except that you will be tuning the open fourth string to the fifth fret of the fifth string to find the correct pitch.

Step Three: Do it again, tuning the open third string to the note produced by pressing down on the fifth fret of the fourth string.

Step Four: This one is different. You are going to tune the open second string to the fourth fret of the third string.

And lastly, it's back to the pattern of Step One: Tune the open first string to the fifth fret of the second string.

Once you have completed this process, your guitar should be in tune. Don't be discouraged if it doesn't sound like a perfect success the first few times you try it. You'll get better with practice. Besides, you can always go back to your electronic tuner!

Keep in mind these final notes about tuning:

When you change strings, it can be very frustrating because the new strings will stretch and continually go out of tune until they have stretched out completely, especially nylon strings.

At times guitarists will say something like "Give me an A" when they are tuning to another guitar because the A string (fifth string open) is the easiest one to do this with when beginning to tune using the traditional method.

Sometimes a guitar will be in pitch when you play open strings but out of tune when you play a chord higher on the neck like on the fifth or seventh fret. This is a sign you should have a guitar technician make the needed adjustment in the neck.

Because guitars are constantly getting out of tune, a guitarist needs to become an expert tuner. (It's not like playing a piano and hiring someone to come tune it once a year.) You must tune your guitar every time you play, and even while you are playing, you may have to retune several times. Guitars get out of tune for many reasons such as strings stretching, temperature changing, tuning pegs slipping, etc. Even one string that is just slightly off will make a chord sound terrible.

The Basis of All Songs: Playing Chords

Chords are the essence of guitar playing. No matter how many years you play or how accomplished you become, chords will always be an important reference point for you. After you have learned to tune your guitar, you should begin to get familiar with some basic chords.

Chords are the basis of songs. If you learn a few chords, get the fingering down, can produce a clear sound from the strings, and practice so you can change the chords quickly, you will soon be able to play hundreds of songs.

Start by learning to play nine basic chords: A, C, D, E, F, G, Am, Dm and Em. These chords sound wonderful and are used in many songs. They are also great to start with because they are relatively easy to play. Even if it doesn't seem this way at first, a little practice will quickly make them friendlier—that's a promise.

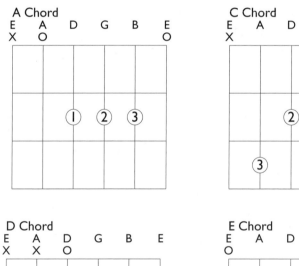

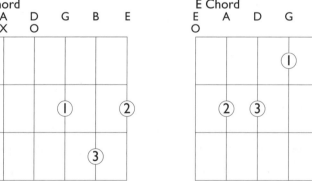

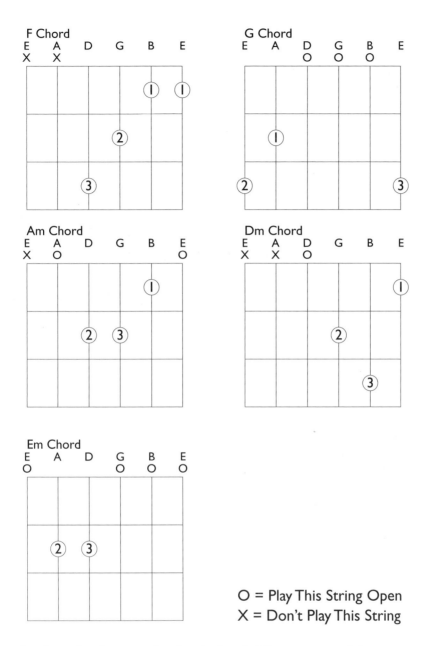

F Chord

E	A	D	G	B	E
X	X				

G Chord

E	A	D	G	B	E
		O	O	O	

Am Chord

E	A	D	G	B	E
X	O				O

Dm Chord

E	A	D	G	B	E
X	X	O			

Em Chord

E	A	D	G	B	E
O			O	O	O

O = Play This String Open

X = Don't Play This String

Look at the diagram for the A chord. The six vertical lines represent the strings of your guitar. The line on the far left is the E (sixth string, the thickest one). The next line to the right represents the A (fifth string). The next line is the D (fourth string), followed by the G (third), B (second) and finally the E (first string, the thinnest one, on the far right).

Now look at the horizontal lines in the A chord diagram. The top line represents the nut of the guitar at the top of the neck. The three lines below it line represent the metal fret bars running across the neck.

Notice that the A chord has the numbers 1, 2, and 3 sitting between the second and third horizontal lines. These numbers represent the 1, 2 and 3 fingers of your left (chording) hand. What the diagram is saying is that you should press down those fingers on the strings and frets indicated.

To play an A chord, place your first finger on the second fret of the fourth string, then your second finger on the second fret of the third string, and finally your third finger on the second fret of the second string.

(Note: A "fret" is the space in between the metal bars that run across the neck of the guitar. For example, if you press your first finger on the string between the nut and the first metal bar, it will be on the first fret. If you move your finger up and press between the first metal bar and the second bar, this would be the second fret, etc.)

Notice that on the diagram of the A chord, the first and fifth strings have an "o" sitting above the nut. This means the string should be played "open"—without pressing down on any fret at all. These open strings are important parts of the chord.

Above the nut on the sixth string is an "x." This means "do not play" this string as part of the chord. You will play only the first five strings but not the sixth when strumming.

This is the basic way to read a chord diagram. It will tell you when to place your fingers on the strings for all the remaining chords.

Sometimes students ask what makes a chord sound good. What is the music theory behind the formation of chords? Actually, it is quite simple.

C is a good key to examine as an example because there are no sharps or flats. The notes are: C-D-E-F-G-A-B-C, with the last C an octave higher than the first.

The chord formula for a major chord is 1-3-5. This means that if you take the first, third and fifth notes in the key of C (C-E-G) and combine them in any order, the result will always be a C chord.

You can see that even though the frets and shapes, or inversions, of the C chords in the illustration are different, what they have in common is that they all combine C-E-G notes, and thus are all C chords.

These inversions, the different ways of playing the chord, can be substituted for one other depending on which C chord sounds best to you.

This is the logic behind how all chords are created, following the same formula which gives them their name and sound. Though there are many different chord formula combinations, it will be sufficient for us now to consider just the major, minor, and 7th chords.

Just as there is a major chord formula (1-3-5), there is one for the minor chords as well (1-b3-5). In the key of C, this would be C-Eb-G, as the illustration shows. Using the 7th chord formula, 1-3-5-♭7 in the key of C would be C-E-G-B♭.

C major, C minor, C7 Chords with Notes Identified

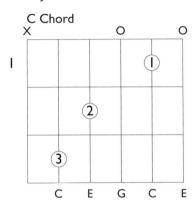

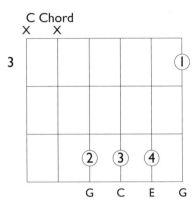

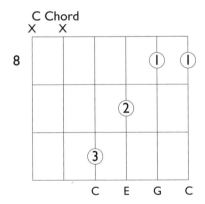

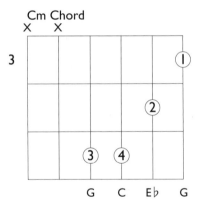

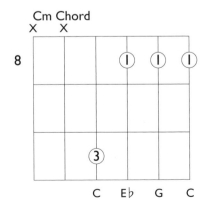

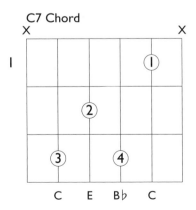

C major, C minor, C7 Chords with Notes Identified (continued)

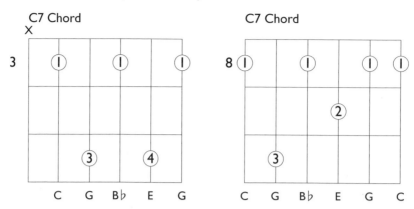

C7 Chord

C7 Chord

Here are some basic tips for playing chords:

Hand position is very important. Make sure your fingers are coming down vertically on the strings your chording hand is pressing down on.

Another key point about hand position is keeping the thumb on your chording hand near the middle to top part of the back of the neck. This will ensure good finger position. Do not let your thumb hang over the top of the neck.

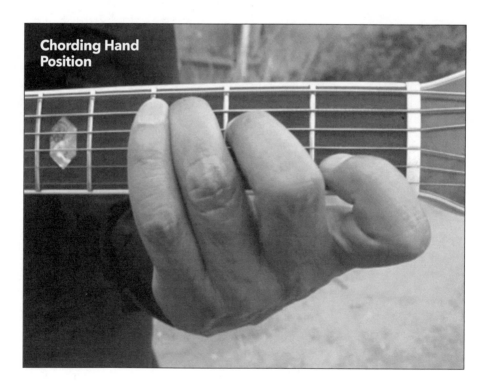

Chording Hand Position

As you hold down a chord, there should be a gap in the space between your thumb and first finger as they wrap around the guitar neck. Do not let the fleshy web between your thumb and first finger touch the guitar neck.

Chording Hand Thumb Position

Also pay attention to the position of your guitar when you are holding it. Keep it upright with a very slight backward tilt so that you can look down at the front. Often, beginning guitarists will tilt their guitar too far backward to get a better view of their chords and fingers. This causes the wrist and chording hand to uncomfortably contort in adjusting to the resulting awkward angle.

Guitar Neck Hand Position

Holding the Guitar

Make sure your fingers are on the right strings and frets when playing a chord. If you are not getting a clean sound from every string in the chord, and instead are hearing a "thump" or a "buzz," you may not be pressing down hard enough on a string, or you might be accidentally touching a neighboring string with a finger that is helping to make the chord, thus dampening the other string and not letting it vibrate.

If you are doing everything right and still not getting a pleasant, harmonious sound, double check to make sure your guitar is in tune.

Once you can play these nine chords in a way that sounds good, the next thing to work on is changing the chords quickly. The goal is to make it almost instantaneous; the rhythm of a song will not wait for you to change chords. When you lift your fingers from a chord, they should be forming the next one above the neck, and then should all land together to shape it. There is no time to form chords one finger at a time.

It is also too cumbersome to look at a chord diagram and then watch your fingers form the chord. You should remember the chords in your fingers' muscle memory so that playing them becomes as natural and effortless as signing your name—even with your eyes closed or in the dark.

A good way to practice, especially if your fingers are sore or you want to practice quietly, is to work on just lifting your fingers and having them land on the neck in the shape of complete chords but without pressing down.

The chords will all become easier as your fingers become more agile through practice. Chords that you can't play now will eventually become playable—and even musical—with repetition and effort. Pick a song and keep working on it until you can change the chords easily and quickly. This will give you the motivation to keep going. It is much more interesting to practice songs than only chords.

The first thing people will often ask when you tell them you are learning to play the guitar is, "What can you play?" Learn the chords to a simple song—find them by just typing into Google—so you have an answer for them. Many guitar books teach beginning guitarists notes and theory but don't get around to teaching them how to play anything they can show off. This can be very discouraging.

Discovering Your Inner Beat: Strumming

Strumming ability coincides with a sense of rhythm, which is something most guitarists naturally possess. In many ways, you cannot teach a person "how to strum." It usually helps more to give the player a sense of confidence that he or she can strum instinctively. This sense of freedom will encourage the guitarist's natural feeling for rhythm and help in expressing it.

The most important rule about strumming is that there are no rules. Beginning guitarists often make the mistake of trying to strum too precisely, exactly on beat, and this has the effect of making their strumming seem wooden and stiff. Good strumming "breaths." It wanders off beat at times and then falls back in. Interesting strumming is messy. Listen to musicians like the Rolling Stones and Bob Dylan as examples. They have no problem wandering off-beat at times and throwing in unusual rhythms at various places in a song.

You may want to think of the guitar as a drum, with the guitar pick being a drumstick and the strings as the head of the drum. Try strumming the same way you would keep a beat with a drumstick, using your pick for both up and down strokes.

Make your strokes wide with a large sweeping motion. Strum from the top of the guitar's body to the bottom. Your arm should be as loose as possible, almost like a rubber band. As it's going up and down, your wrist should be turning smoothly from side to side. Hold the pick loosely between your fingers with your thumb gripping about half of it on one side and your first finger holding about half on the other side. Have your first finger curl in a little toward your palm.

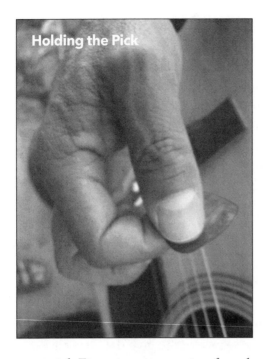

Holding the Pick

When you hold the pick, keep it loosely between your thumb and first finger so that you brush the strings when you strum them rather than pounding on them. Discover how tightly you need to hold the pick without letting it slip out of your fingers.

Strum the guitar in the area of the sound hole closer to the bridge. This is where you will generally find the best tone.

Here are a couple of exercises that may help you capture your strumming potential. First, turn your guitar face down. Think about a song that you want to strum and act as if you were a drummer, tapping out the beat with your strumming hand on the back of the guitar. When you have done this for a while, hold the guitar as you normally would to play it and keep the same beat with down and up strokes on the strings. This will help you think of your guitar strumming in the same way a drummer would focus on keeping a beat.

A second exercise is to listen to one of your favorite recordings and once again think of your guitar as a drum, keeping the beat to the music with up and down strokes across the strings. Instead of making chords, hold your left hand over the strings, lightly touching them so that no sound comes out. And actually, with no sound, your guitar truly is a drum. Be imaginative and bold, and try adding other strokes mixed in. When you have done this for a while, go back to playing your chords, and you will find that you have a much freer, more imaginative style of strumming.

Finding Notes on the Guitar

Knowing the notes on your guitar neck is helpful for a number of reasons. Besides letting you follow written sheet music, being able to locate notes will help you with naming chords, playing lead guitar, writing songs, and figuring out the chords to songs you wish to play.

To begin identifying notes on the guitar, start by memorizing the notes that are produced by the six open strings. When your guitar is properly tuned to standard tuning, these will be the notes made by your open strings:

Open Strings Notes

Sixth string—E   Fourth string—D   Second string—B
Fifth string—A   Third string—G   First string—E

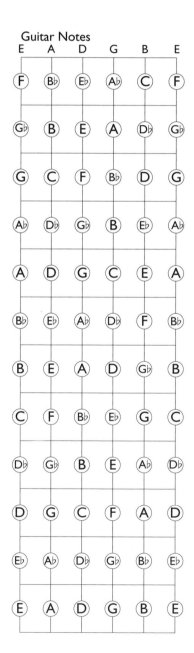

Let's look at the sequence of notes:

A—B♭ (or A#), B—C—D♭ (or C#), D—E♭ (or D#), E—F—G♭ (or F#), G—A♭ (or G#)

In guitar language, think of notes this way:

♭ = flat = one fret lower in pitch

= sharp = one fret higher in pitch

You will notice that some notes have two names like G♭ (or F#). This is because you can get to the same note on the same fret in two ways. For example, a G♭ or F# on the second fret of the first string can be reached by sharping (#) the F note on the first fret by one fret or flatting (b) the G note on the third fret by one fret. Either way, you end up on the second fret.

With what you have learned, you should now be able to name every note on your guitar neck. Granted, not very quickly yet but given enough time, you can do it.

Chords Are Not Set in Stone: Altering Chords

Once you become more comfortable with the basic chords—A, C, D, E, F, G, Am, Dm, and Em—it is time to begin looking at them in a different light. Think of these chords as fluid rather than set in stone. You can create some very interesting sounds simply by adding or lifting a finger in relation to the original chord.

Let's start with the D chord. Lift your second finger from the second fret of the first string and play the first string open as you strum the D chord. By lifting the second finger, you are adding a different flavor to your D chord.

Now put your second finger back where it was when you played the original D chord. This time take your fourth finger and place it on the third fret of the first string, above your second finger. Now strum this chord. This is another way of altering your D chord.

Experiment and alternate between the original D chord and these two variations. You may hear something that reminds you of songs you've heard before. You can get some nice sounds from playing altered chords.

A question you may ask is: Are these altered chords still a D chord despite the changes I made? Technically, no they aren't, but most guitarists don't worry about this; they just think of them as D chords modified a bit.

Below are some common alterations that are often made to some of the chords you've already learned. Play with these alterations and have fun with them. They will make your chord playing more interesting. You can even create some of your own. Try new things. No "Guitar Police" will show up and tell you that you can't mess with the chords. You have nothing to lose by being creative.

Altered Chords

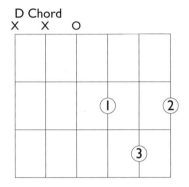

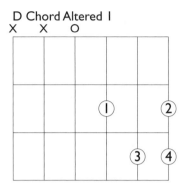

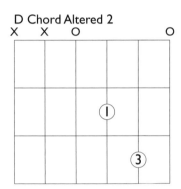

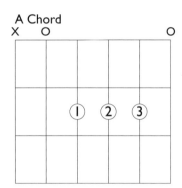

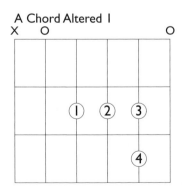

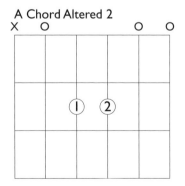

Altered Chords (continued)

E Chord
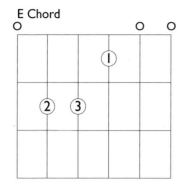

E Chord Altered 1
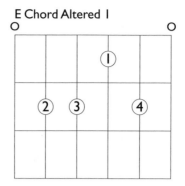

E Chord Altered 2
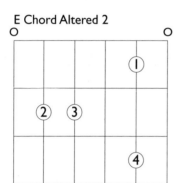

Am Chord
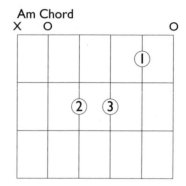

Am Chord Altered 1
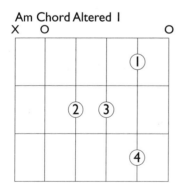

Am Chord Altered 2
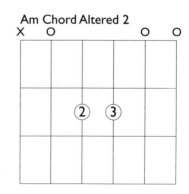

Altered Chords (continued)

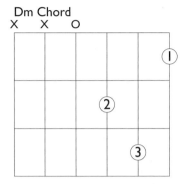

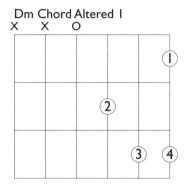

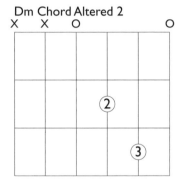

Focusing on the Bottom: Bass Notes

Emphasizing bass notes in chord playing is a basic technique that is important in a variety of musical styles. Whether you are strumming or fingerpicking, focusing on bass notes can make a big difference. You can begin examining bass notes by looking at the nine basic chords A, C, D, E, F, G, Am, Dm, and Em.

The lowest-sounding two strings in the chord usually will be the bass notes. For example, the E chord has the A (fifth) string and the E (sixth) string as its bass notes since they are the lowest two strings in the chord. The C chord has the D (fourth) string and the A (fifth) as its lowest strings and bass notes, since the E (sixth) string, which has an "x" over it, is not played.

Traditionally, the second lowest string in the chords is the "first bass note" and the lowest string the "second bass note." For example, with the A chord, the D string is the first bass note and the A string is the second bass note.

Bass Notes on Lower Strings of Basic Chords

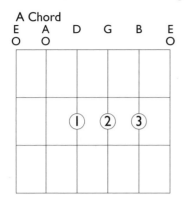

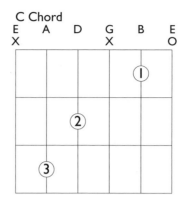

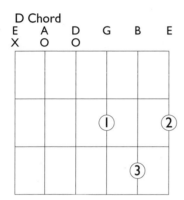

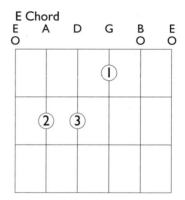

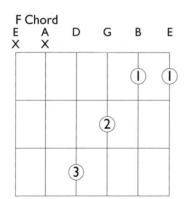

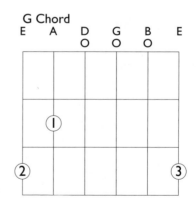

Bass Notes on Lower Strings of Basic Chords (continued)

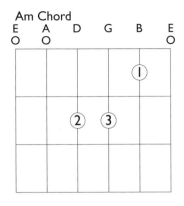

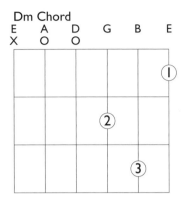

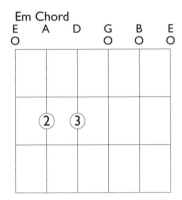

Using a pick, play a bass note strumming pattern by hitting the first bass note and strumming downward twice on the strings below the bass note. Next, play the second bass note and strum down twice (either with or without the first base note string). Keep repeating the pattern during chord changes.

• 1-strum, strum/2 strum, strum. (This is a pattern common in many country and folk songs.)

Two other variations are:

• 1-strum/2-strum (common in many folk songs).

• 1-strum, strum, strum/2 strum-strum-strum (common in bluegrass and folk songs). Do this with down-up-down strum strokes.

The use of bass notes in fingerpicking is also very important and will be discussed later in the fingerpicking section.

When playing a chord, keep in mind that you can choose bass notes from any of the lower notes in a chord, usually the ones located on the fourth, fifth, and sixth strings. Experiment with different chords and strums, and remember that there are no hard-and-fast rules.

Putting All Those Fingers to Work: Fingerpicking

Fingerpicking is a popular technique in various styles of music. The key to learning it is to train your fingers to act instinctively and move independently. Every song you play will require its own fingerpicking accompaniment, and this has to be done on an unconscious, spontaneous level. One good step to get to the point where your fingers can "think for themselves" is learning some basic picking patterns. Think of them as training for your fingers. And in addition, they actually sound very nice and can be used in many playing situations. Keep in mind that eventually, although you can insert a fingerpicking pattern anyplace in a song, you will not want to depend on the same repetitive pattern through the entire song.

Pattern 1:

Finger: T – 3 – 1 – 2

String: 4 – 1 – 3 – 2

This pattern progresses from left to right in the order below:

Your thumb picks the fourth string, third finger picks the first string, first finger picks the third string, and second finger picks the second string.

Practice this pattern until you can play it smoothly without thinking about it. Your fingers should be placed around the middle to bottom half of the sound hole for the best tone. Start slowly and increase your speed as the pattern becomes more natural. Keep the tempo consistent: 1,2,3,4; 1,2,3,4 . . .

This pattern is very good practice for your fingers because it uses all the picking fingers on your right hand (since the fourth finger is not very useful for picking). It also requires you to practice a pattern that is complex enough to make you concentrate.

Try keeping the pattern going as you change chords. Once you can do this fairly easily, try to change the pattern this way:

Alternate your thumb between the fourth string and the fifth to create an alternating bass line. This will give your picking pattern a feeling of movement. You can refer back to the section on bass notes for string possibilities to play with your thumb. With some chords, you may alternate between the fourth and fifth strings, and with other chords, use the fifth and sixth strings for the bass notes.

The second fingerpick style to learn is called "Travis picking" (named after the early country music star Merle Travis). It's a technique that has traditionally been passed down from guitarist to guitarist at bluegrass and folk festivals. We'll use what's called tablature, or tab, to learn it.

"Travis Picking" chart

Finger positions: Thumb starts on root note, fingers 1,2 and 3 on bottom three strings.

Travis Pick on 6 Strings: Try G or Em Chords

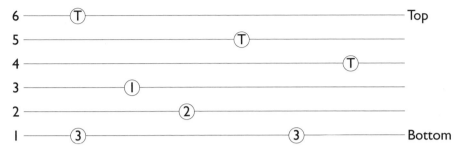

Travis Pick on 5 Strings: Try C or Am Chords

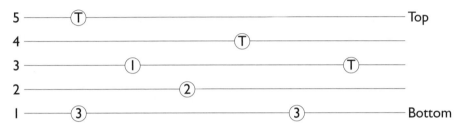

Travis Pick on 4 Strings: Try D or F Chords

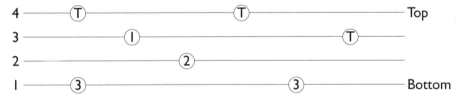

Rhythm 4/4 Time: one, two-and, three-and, four

The way to read this tablature is to think of the six lines in the figure as the strings of a guitar. Just as when you're looking over the top of your guitar while holding it, the top (thickest) string is the sixth string, and the lowest (thinnest) string is your first.

The tablature for the Travis pick indicates that you begin by hitting the sixth string with your T finger (thumb) and simultaneously pick the first string with your third finger; in other words, you will play the first and sixth strings at the same time.

Continuing along from left to right, you pick the third string with your first finger, followed by the second string with your second finger. Then your T finger plays the fifth string, the third finger hits the first string, and the T finger plays the fourth string.

The rhythm you want for this pattern is "one, two-and, three-and, four."

This picking pattern is the tab you would use for a six-string chord like a G or Em chord.

For five-string chords like C or Am, the pattern would change slightly to leave out the sixth string: Instead, pick the fifth, fourth, and third strings with your thumb, all else remains the same.

For four-string chords like D or F, you omit the fifth and sixth strings, picking the fourth string twice and the third string with your thumb; all else remains the same.

Practice this pattern until it becomes smooth and natural. Start slowly and make sure you're hitting the right strings with the right fingers; then slowly increase the speed as you grow more confident.

Try to keep the pick going as you change among four-string, five-string, and six-string chords.

As I mentioned earlier, these fingerpicking patterns sound great unaltered. But their main purpose is to train your fingers, not to make you a slave to the patterns after you have mastered them. Once you can play these picks easily, you will find your fingers doing unconscious variations on them. This is good! It means your fingers are beginning to think for themselves. Every song you play will dictate its own picking style, which will be slightly different from any other song's.

If you ask any good fingerpicker how he or she played a particular song, the answer will be, "I don't know; I just did it." The guitarist isn't being coy or hiding some technique from you. The playing really was on an instinctive level. That's what good fingerpickers do!

The final technique I will offer is a simple but important one. It has the same setup as the first pick in this section:

Finger: T – 3 – 1 – 2
String: 4 – 1 – 3 – 2

But instead of picking the strings in order, pluck all four simultaneously. This will break up your picking patterns so that they don't become too repetitive. When you change to a new chord, try to occasionally pluck all the strings in this way and then go back to your original fingerpicking pattern. It will make your playing much more interesting and unpredictable.

Becoming a Chord Monster: Barre and Movable Chords

Once you have mastered the basic chords that most beginning guitarists learn—moving among them smoothly while being able to make them sound clear—it is time to expand your horizons and explore movable and barre chords. This will represent a great leap forward in your chord-playing ability and let you multiply the number of chords you can use.

Movable Chords

Movable chords change depending on what fret you're playing on even though your hand position stays the same. For example, a B♭ movable chord that starts on the first fret becomes a B when you begin it on the second fret, a C on the third, a D♭ on the fourth, a D on the fifth, etc.— all with the exact same hand position.

An F movable chord is a G♭ when you play it on the second fret, a G on the third, a A♭ on the fourth, and a A on the fifth, etc. And you haven't changed your fingering to do this!

Similarly, the B♭ minor movable chord on the first fret becomes Bm on the second fret, Cm on the third, D♭m on the fourth, Dm on the

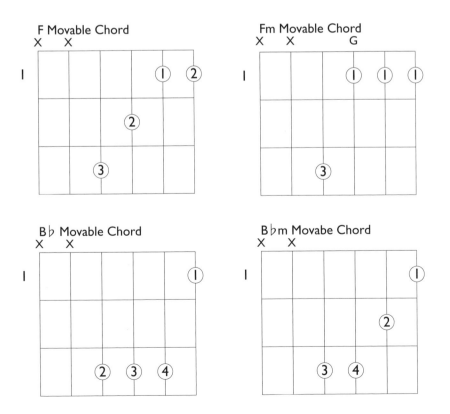

fifth, etc. And the F minor movable chord on the first fret can be moved up the neck to be G♭m on the second fret, Gm on the third, A♭m on the fourth, Am on the fifth, etc.

Barre Chords

The only difference between a barre chord and other movable chords is that a barre chord has the first finger holding down all the strings across the neck and a movable chord does not necessarily have this.

A movable chord, whether a barre chord or not, must not have an open string in it; every string in the chord must be held down. A chord with an open string cannot be moved up the neck because the open string doesn't change like the rest of the chord does as it moves from one fret to another.

The chord diagrams below show the major, minor, and 7th barre chords on the first fret—all of them F chords.

Major Barre Chord

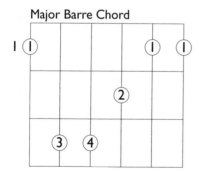

Minor Barre Chord

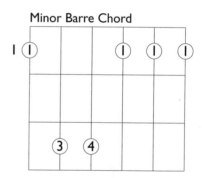

7th Barre Chord

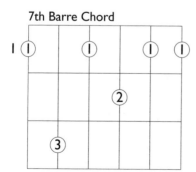

They become Gb on the second fret, G on the third, Ab on the fourth, A on the fifth, Bb on the sixth, B on the seventh fret, C on the eighth, Db on the 9th, D on the tenth, Eb on the eleventh, and E on the twelfth fret.

The chord diagrams below show the major, minor, and 7th barre chords on the first fret—all of them Bb chords.

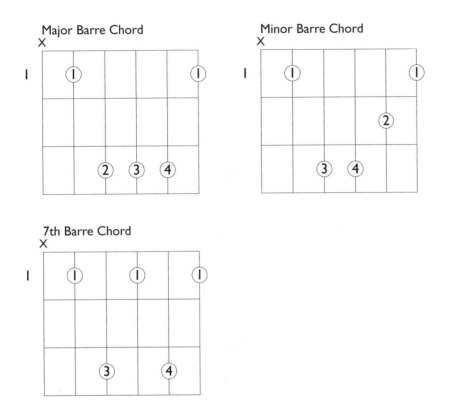

These are Bb chords on the first fret, then B on the second, C on the third, Db on the fourth, D on the fifth, Eb on the sixth, E on the seventh fret, F on the eighth, Gb on the ninth fret, G on the tenth, Ab on the eleventh, and A on the twelfth fret.

Perhaps you have wondered why the first nine chords you learned are all on the first three frets and professional guitarists you see are playing chords all over the neck. This is because they are playing a variety of barre and movable chords.

The key to playing barre chords is to be able to hold down all the strings with your first finger. When you can do this, they are also a big help because it takes only a minor finger adjustment to create a major, minor, or 7th chord.

Clearly, playing barre chords means you must develop a first finger strong enough to press down on all six strings at the same time. To do that, you need to pay attention to some basic techniques:

Your thumb should be placed near the middle of the back of the neck so that pressure is applied from both the thumb in back and the finger in front, just like a vice works. The first finger should extend across the fret with a natural curve at the knuckle, meaning you don't keep your finger rigidly straight to hold down the strings.

Let the tip of your first finger extend past the sixth string so that the bottom of your fingernail lines up with the sixth string.

When you press down on the strings, you should roll your first finger so you're using the side of the finger closest to the thumb, rather than the flat part, to press down with. Pulling your left elbow in toward your side until it touches your left rib area will help move your first finger into the right position.

If you can get a clean sound from all six strings when you press down with your first finger; you have accomplished the hardest part of playing barre chords.

Barre Chord Finger Position

The next step is to place the rest of your fingers in position on the adjacent frets as indicated in the chord diagrams.

Though it may seem difficult at first, the barre chord will definitely become easier with time.

You've Got to Be Versatile Man, Part 2: Naming Barre and Movable Chords

To correctly name barre and movable chords, you must first find the "root note" for the chord you are playing. This is the that one gives the chord its name.

F Major Barre Chord

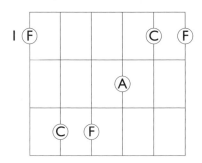

For example, examine the barred major chord illustrated above. The root note can be found at three places in the chord, the first string, the fourth string, and the sixth string. All of these are the same note played in different octaves.

If you barre the major chord on the first fret, the notes on the first, fourth, and sixth strings will all be F's, the root notes in the F major chord.

If you move the chord up one fret so your first finger is barring across the second fret rather that the first, the notes you play on the first, fourth, and sixth strings will no longer be F's but rather Gb notes. With these new root notes, you're playing a G♭ major chord.

If you move the chord up once again so you're barring on the third fret, it becomes a G chord. Barring the fourth fret would create an A♭ chord, the fifth fret an A chord, and so on.

Just follow the notes in order as you go up the neck. This is a very efficient way of playing chords because once you learn one barre major chord, you can instantly create eleven new major chords by simply moving your hand shape up the neck. The F major barre chord illustrated above is the granddaddy of all rock 'n' roll chords; countless songs have been written just by moving it up and down.

To identify the chord you're playing, you can focus on just one of the root notes in the chord, such as the one on the first string for the major barre chord illustrated on page 99. The name of the chord will be the same as the note you are playing on the first string. It's as simple as that.

When a different fret is barred, the F major chord will become:

Second fret—G♭	Seventh—B	Twelfth—E
Third—G	Eighth—C	Thirteenth—F (con-
Fourth—A♭	Ninth—D♭	tinuing the sequence
Fifth—A	Tenth—D	until you run out of
Sixth—B♭	Eleventh-E♭	room on the neck)

Another great aspect of using barre chords is the ease of switching from a major barre chord to a minor or 7th chord. It's literally as easy as lifting a finger, as shown on Page 96.

To make the major chord into a minor chord, all you have to do is lift your second finger, and instantly the chord switches from a major to minor.

To transform the major chord into a 7th, just lift off your fourth finger.

In all these cases, the root notes remain the same. For example, barring on the first fret, the chords would be F major, F minor, and F7. Barring on the second fret, they would be G♭ major, G♭ minor, G♭7, and so on sliding up one fret at a time and following the sequence of notes.

Playing these chords and understanding the basic concepts of barre chords will let you quickly master every major, minor, and 7th chord there is—all thirty-six of them!

The B♭ row of barre chords illustrated on Page 97 also has chords that will be helpful to know, although they are not as widely used as those in the F row. The root notes are on the third and fifth strings for these chords. Based on the starting fret you play, these chords would be:

First fret—B♭	Sixth—E♭	Eleventh—A♭
Second—B	Seventh—E	Twelfth—A
Third—C	Eighth—F	Thirteenth—B♭
Fourth—D♭	Ninth—G♭	
Fifth—D	Tenth—G	

Congratulations! Now you know two ways to play barre chords for all the major, minor, and 7th chords. You have learned seventy-two new chords!

Guitar Musings

Playing the guitar requires several refined skills such as hand-eye coordination, creativity, memory, and intuition. But best of all, it's good for your mental health. It balances and stimulates the mind like nothing else can, calling on both sides of the brain to access creativity as well as structured thinking. But guitarists already know this.

Making music may be older than even speech in human experience. Ever since our ancestors began drumming out basic rhythms or blowing through flutes made of mammoth bone 43,000 years ago, we have been intimately connected to music-making.

People pick up the guitar for many reasons. For some, it's a desire to become performers and show their skills onstage, while for others, guitar playing is a more-personal activity bringing the joy of mastering the instrument's technique and structure.

Playing the guitar can teach us much about life. It is an instrument of infinite possibilities which teaches guitarists to go beyond their boundaries. Learning to interact with and complement others rather than being the center of attention at all times is another valuable lesson. The guitar challenges players to think creatively and solve problems, and emphasizes the importance of living in tune. Every guitarist establishes a unique relationship with his or her guitar, and this is the true gift of music.

*   *   *

You need to build a relationship with your guitar. How much time it sits in your arms is a good measure of how good you will become, not the number of lessons you take or how much you pay for them.

The guitar should be fun. You "play" the guitar; you don't "work" it.

Playing is based on honest effort and skill. You can't BS on the guitar; either you can play the song, or you can't.

You will always be your own harshest critic. You will always be acutely aware of your limitations. Learn to listen to yourself with love and appreciation.

The greats we all admire are people in love with, and obsessed by, the guitar. They're the players the most innovative advances have come from, guitarists like:

• George Harrison, who practiced as a boy until his fingers bled;

• Keith Richards, who wrote in his autobiography, *Life,* that he often fell asleep with his guitar;

• Jimi Hendrix, whose excessive guitar playing—by Army standards—was one of the reasons for his discharge; and

• The many trailblazers—like B.B. King, Muddy Waters, and Chet Atkins—who made their own guitars when they couldn't afford to buy one.

Practice is what develops muscle memory. It is better to do this a little every day than to play for long periods of time on an only-occasional basis. Have your guitar out where you'll bump into it constantly. If you put it in its case back in a closet, you'll be a lot less likely to go through the trouble of taking it out to practice; that's just human nature.

It sometimes helps to have a certain time every day that you devote to practice. This will help make it a habit, and you'll feel there's something missing if you don't touch your guitar at least once a day.

Again, don't work at the guitar; it is not another obligation you're taking on. Once it becomes work, it loses its magic. I have seen very accomplished players, as well as beginners, quit completely because they had this attitude.

Think of playing and practicing as enjoyment rather than a chore. It is not a competitive undertaking; accept your progress as a gradual unfolding that will happen at its own rate—which definitely will not be overnight. Think about how long it took you to master other skills such as reading, writing, or learning a language, and approach guitar playing with this in mind.

When you practice, don't play only what you already know or repeat what you can do well. Continually practice new things and stretch yourself. Work on pieces and skills that are hard for you. This is the best way to improve and not get bored with your own playing. In other words, don't play just what is easy but also address your weaknesses. When you are a beginner, your progress can be dramatic, and exciting. However, as you improve, it will come more slowly, and you will have to try harder to see it. That's just the way it is.

*   *   *

A good guitar teacher can be worth his or her weight in gold. Putting your money into lessons rather than a fancy guitar will take you a lot further. If you're getting bored with your own playing, this a sign it's time for lessons.

As with any other endeavor, you've got to have the right tools to do the job. This means a playable guitar with reasonable action and intonation. But don't make the mistake of putting all your money into your instrument; leave some for guitar lessons. You are the main musical conduit.

*   *   *

It is important to consider the quality of the guitar you are playing as you begin to practice. You don't need an instrument that's outlandishly expensive, but if it doesn't have some basic qualities, you'll be fighting an uphill battle in your quest to play the guitar. A subpar instrument will make it difficult if not impossible for your playing to advance.

It cannot be overemphasized that a guitar must be capable of being tuned and remaining in tune. If your guitar isn't in tune, nothing you try to play will sound good, and sour-sounding notes will quickly diminish your enthusiasm.

Usually, a guitar's tuning problems can be traced to one of three causes: tuning keys that are slipping or defective in some other way; a bowed or warped neck (which can cost more to repair than the instrument is worth); or strings that are simply too old and need to be replaced with a set that will hold the pitch.

*   *   *

The possibilities that the neck of the guitar give you are infinite; no one can completely master the instrument. Even if a player were to gain proficiency in one genre, it would take more than a lifetime to command the many other styles such as classical, blues, jazz, folk, etc. But as you go through the happy task of learning as much as you can, here are some thoughts to keep in mind:
  • Learn from the masters, but create your own original style.
  • Leave your ego at the door. How many bands have broken up over ego?

• Don't quit your day job. The old blues players used to call the guitar the "starvation box" for a reason. Music is a tough way to make a living. All the thousands of towns in America have their guitar heroes—in many ways just as talented as rich and famous musicians, yet the vast majority will never "make it big." Don't play for fame and fortune; rather, play because you love it, and you will never be disappointed.

* * *

Don't give up! Think about the first time you tried anything new. For instance, if you ever took up a new sport such as tennis, did you hit the ball like Roger Federer immediately? Did you make ten free throws in a row the first time you shot a basketball? Did you speak fluent Spanish after your first class? The same principle applies to playing the guitar. You must be patient with yourself and your progress. Even Segovia and Clapton had to struggle with their first chords.

* * *

The first chords you learn and practice are commonly the easiest to play. But don't make the mistake of thinking that makes them in any way inferior to or less worthy than more-complex chords. A rose is not less beautiful than a tulip because it is considered less exotic.

This is a subject on which I have a confession to make. Several years ago, I was in the midst of some very intense guitar study, and I got caught in the mental trap of thinking that more complex and difficult technique somehow equated to "better" guitar playing. Slowly, this attitude began to erode my enjoyment of the guitar. Playing became a competitive endeavor rather than the heart-centered, creative act that had seduced me when I first started. Once I turned it into a dry, intellectual challenge, I was not having much fun anymore, and playing began to lose its "juice." More than a few guitarists—as well as other musicians, painters, writers, and people doing all kinds of creative work—also have become enamored with technique and complexity, dampening the very inspiration and joy that drew them to take up their art in the first place.

To make a long story short, I became "burned out," and didn't pick up my guitar again for several months. It had become an obligation, another goal that I would ultimately fall short of. It was another disappointment in my quest for mastery and perfection in my world of limitations.

Then one day after my hiatus of neglect, I summoned the will to pick up my guitar again, and I held it, wondering what to play. The first thing my fingers gravitated to was a basic D chord, one of the first chords I had ever learned. I strummed it, and its sound was a revelation. This simple chord was beautiful in its composition; in fact, it was perfect. This chord which millions of guitar players know and use daily needed no improvement or coloring. I felt like I was back in touch with the mother lode. I was listening to this chord the same way I had the first time I played it.

The awe-inspiring combination of notes sounded fresh and alive. I no longer took it for granted or needed to elaborate on it. I was starting over! Blessed simplicity! My ego was no longer in charge; the music was in control again.

Index

Photographs and fingering charts are designated by the page number in *italics*.

About the Author

Andrew Leo Lovato has been a lover of the guitar and the blues since he first made their acquaintance fifty years ago. He has taught guitar classes in Santa Fe for the past thirty years, and estimates that in that time, he has taught more than a thousand adults and children to play the guitar (which comes to about 1 out of every 80 people in the city).

He is currently a professor of communication and music at Santa Fe Community College, and has developed courses including "Popular Music and Communication" and "The Cultural Roots of Creativity." He received his Ph.D. from the University of New Mexico in 2000, is the author of several books on the history and culture of New Mexico, and also was a popular music radio D.J. for ten years in the 1970s and '80s.

Lovato was chosen as a Fulbright Scholar in 2008 and has served as Santa Fe's official City Historian. He lives in Tesuque, New Mexico, a small village about seven miles north of Santa Fe, with his wife, Anhara, and their dog, three cats, and numerous rabbits and chickens.